MEDITERRANEAN SEA

ASIA MINOR

PERSIA

A

Beirut

Alexandria Port Said
Suez

EGYPT

RED SEA

PERSIAN GULF

Karachi

IN

ARABIA

Muscat

ARABIAN SEA

Bomba

Perim
Aden

Socotra

⚓ 11

Laccadive Is.

C

Djibouti

Berbera

Cape Guardafui

NINE DEGREE CHANNEL

ABYSSINIA

MINICOY

Colo

Maldive Is.

KENYA
COLONY

Mombasa

Seychelles Is. ..

⚓ 5

Pemba

⚓ 12

Dar-es-Salaam Zanzibar

Amirante Is.

⚓ 7

Chagos Arch

TANGANYIKA
TERRITORY

Aldabra Is.

Providence Is.

Saya de Malha Bank

⚓ 6 Diego

Diégo Suarez

Nazareth Bank

Mozambique

Caragados
Carajos
Rodriguez

UNION OF
SOUTH
AFRICA

Beira

Tromelin Is.

MADAGASCAR

Europa Is.

St. Denis

Mauritius

Réunion

Lourenço Marques

Delagoa Bay

Port Nolloth

⚓ 3

Durban

Port Elizabeth East London
Cape Town

Mossel Bay

Key to the posi

1	Augustina
2	Ondina
3	Elysia
4	Daisy Moller
5	British Chiva
6	Sutlej
7	Ascot

I A

Taku
Chefoo

KOREA

SEA OF JAPAN

JAPAN

Yokohama

Nagasaki

Shanghai

CHINA

Foochow
Amoy

Swatow

Nansei Shoto

Ogasawara

alcutta   Chittagong

Haiphong

Hong Kong   BASHI CHANNEL

BALINTANG CHANNEL

BAY OF
BENGAL

Rangoon

THAILAND

CHINA SEA   Manila

SAN BERNARDINO STRAIT

Mariana Is.

4

Andaman Is.

dras

Bangkok

Nicobar Is.   Mergui

rincomalee

GULF
OF
THAILAND

Saigon

SUNGAO STRAIT

3atticaloa   We Is.

LON

BENGAL PASSAGE

MALACCA STRAIT

Penang

Singapore

BASILAN STRAIT

CARIMATA STRAIT

PALAWAN PASSAGE

MOLUCCA PASSAGE

SUMATRA

BANKA STR.

GASPAR STR.

Borneo

MAKASSA STRAIT

DJAILOLO PASSAGE

Celebes

NEW GUINEA

13

STRAAT SOENDA

JAVA   JAVA SEA

Ceram

MANIPA STRAIT

Christmas Is.   BALI STR.   Timor

Cocos or Keeling Is.   LOMBOK STR.   ALAS. STR.   LOMBAL STRAIT

Great Barrier Reef

TORESS STRAIT

Thursday Is.

1

ARAFURA SEA   P. Darwin

Roebuck Bay

Townsville

8   2

WESTERN
AUSTRALIA

QUEENSLAND

AUSTRALIA

he ships sunk

SOUTH AUSTRALIA

NEW SOUTH WALES

Behar

Fremantle

Nancy Moller

C. Leeuwin

Adelaide

.0   Tjisalak

Albany

.1   Richard Hovey

Melbourne

2   Jean Nicolet

3   Langkoeas

Cape Otway

BLOOD & BUSHIDO

Bernard Edwards

Other books by Bernard Edwards:

Masters Next to God
They Sank the Red Dragon
The Fighting Tramps
The Grey Widow Maker
SOS, Men Against the Sea
Attack & Sink

BLOOD & BUSHIDO

Bernard Edwards

Brick Tower Press
New York

in conjunction with
Bernard Edwards

First US Edition
Brick Tower Press, 1997

© Bernard Edwards, 1991

Edwards, Bernard
Blood & Bushido
Includes Index

ISBN 1-883283-18-3

Library of Congress
Catalog Card Number 97-72347

Bernard Edwards

AUTHOR'S NOTE

This book is factually correct, being based on material supplied by British, American and Dutch naval sources, by the few survivors who remain, and relatives who remember. In reconstructing each incident I have taken great care to adhere to the facts, at the same time drawing on my own experience in these waters, to paint an authentic picture for the reader as each drama unfolds. In no case have I set out to weave a deliberate web of fantasy, but if I have at times paraphrased too liberally, then I crave the indulgence of those concerned.

Bernard Edwards
Llanvaches 1991

For those who died and those who were left to grieve.

"They are all gone into the world of light!
And I alone sit ling'ring here;
Their very memory is fair and bright,
And my sad thoughts doth clear."

–Henry Vaughan, Friends Departed.

PREFACE

At the height of the Battle of the Nile, in August 1798, the French
flagship L'Orient, reeling under Nelson's guns, caught fire and
blew up. Many of her crew were killed outright, but a number jumped
or were blown overboard, to end up half-dazed, clinging to spars and
scraps of wreckage. In the heat of the battle still raging, it might have
been expected the British seamen would have given little thought to
the enemy struggling in the water. Only moments before, the
L'Orient's guns had been pouring shot into the attacking British ships,
killing, maiming and destroying. Nelson, on board the Vanguard, had
himself been seriously wounded, almost losing the sight of his one
remaining eye, yet he too showed concern for the beaten foe. On hearing of the plight of the L'Orient's men, the Admiral staggered up on
deck and ordered boats to be lowered to pick up survivors. Seventy
French seamen were saved through this humane act.

In rescuing the Frenchmen, Horatio Nelson was acting in accordance with a law of the sea which, although unwritten, is unequivocal
and binding. If any man is in distress on the high seas, irrespective of

his nationality, it is the bounden duty of all seamen in the vicinity to do their utmost to save him. Even in war this rule holds good: when the guns have stopped firing, the victor has a moral obligation to go to the aid of the vanquished, putting to one side all that has passed between them.

During World War II, the Allied navies, wherever and whenever humanly possible, exercised this traditional magnanimity towards a beaten enemy. There are many recorded instances of Allied seamen risking their own lives to save those with whom they had been previously locked in a fight to the death. The German U-boat campaign against Allied merchant ships was particularly ruthless and dirty, yet U-boat commanders often surfaced after sinking a ship to give what help they could to survivors. This usually amounted to no more than a course to steer for the land, a few tins of cigarettes or bandages for the wounded, but it was a gesture of solidarity between seamen. Both sides realised the war was only a passing phase and their real, and common enemy, was the sea.

The Japanese Imperial Navy saw things in a very different light, and lost no time in demonstrating this. Three days after Pearl Harbor, on 10 December 1941, the Panamanian flagship Donerail, carrying nothing more threatening than a cargo of sugar and pineapples, was torpedoed south of Hawaii by the Japanese submarine I-10, commanded by Lieutenant Commander Y. Kayahara. The Donerail's crew of 43 escaped in the boats but were, for no apparent reason, summarily machine-gunned by Kayahara. Only 16 survived.

The Donerail was the first of a long line of atrocities. It has been claimed that the Japanese High Command issued an order to its commanders at sea that all survivors of merchant ships sunk should be exterminated. While such an order may be cited as an excuse for these heinous crimes, it does not explain why the executions were carried out with such obvious relish and efficiency. A look back at Japanese history may provide a clue.

Legend has it the people of Japan are descended from the Shinto sun goddess Amaterasu Omikami, and the islands they inhabit were the outcome of a union between the god Izanagai and the goddess Izanami. Japan and its peoples, in the eyes of many, are therefore divine. Certainly, they have one of the oldest known civilisations, and the Imperial line, reputed to have been founded by the Yamato family in 660 BC, is today still unbroken. The many islands which make up the country straddle the northern Pacific for a distance of two thousand miles in a north-east, south-west direction and are mountainous and heavily wooded. Their delicate beauty is such that it is easy to imagine that here the hands of the gods have been at work.

Although no greater in area than the British Isles, due to its elongated configuration, Japan has a climate as varied as any large continent, ranging from cold and wet in the northern island of Hokkaido to sub-tropical in lush Kyushu in the south. Earthquakes are commonplace, and, throughout the months of summer and autumn, typhoons, born in the great open wastes of the Pacific, sweep in to scour the land, cutting wide swathes through forests of sharp-scented pine, devastating towns and villages, and sending ships scuttling for shelter in the fjord-like bays which indent the rocky coast. There is a dark and satanic majesty to the islands of Japan.

Japan is the land of the Shoguns and the Samurai, a land with a long history of internal violence fed by the code of Bushido, which lays down the unassailable rule that death is preferable to dishonour. Yet Japan is also the land of the geisha and the tea ceremony, whose people have, for many centuries, practised the gentle arts. Japanese hand-fashioned pottery is among the earliest known in the world, the world's first novel was written in Japan by Lady Murasaki Shikibu. Caligraphy, flower arrangement and poetry have long been essential ingredients of the Japanese culture. The Japanese smile and bow, even in the face of terrible grief or adversity, and are, on the surface, the most polite race the world has ever known. They are, disciplined, truthful and honorable to a fault, yet they are not deeply religious. They are, at one and the same time, both Buddhists and Shintoists, practising a loose mix of the two religions without embarassment and with a marked lack of hypocrisy. In spite of all this, few foreigners ever get to know the Japanese intimately.

The first Europeans known to have landed in Japan were three Portuguese seamen, shipwrecked in 1543 on Tanega Shima, a tiny island off the south-east tip of Kyushu. Six years later, St Francis Xavier established a small Christian mission at Kagoshima, also in Kyushu. The Portuguese Jesuit found the Japanese to be "people of very good manners, good in general and not malicious." He also observed, "they are men of honour to a marvel, and prize honour above all else in the world."

More than three hundred years were to pass before Japan reluctantly opened its doors to Western trade. In 1853, American naval ships under Commodore Perry blockaded Yokohama, and, at the point of a gun, forced its inhabitants to agree to trade with America. This was the long awaited foot-in-the-door, and the Europeans, Britain in the fore, then hoped to move in and begin empire-building, just as they had done in many other parts of the globe. But their attempts to take over were doomed from the start, for Japan, its islands unoccupied by any foreign power in their long history, was not about to be gathered into the Western fold. The Japanese were, however, astute enough and quick enough to accept and absorb much of the Western technology that now came within their grasp.

Despite being an island race, the Japanese limited their sea-going activities to fishing and travel between the confines of their own islands. It was not until 1863 that they gave serious thought to a navy of their own. In the summer of that year, a British naval squadron bombarded Kagoshima in retaliation for the murder of an English trader and reduced the port to ruins. Contrary to expectations, Japanese reaction was not one of outrage, but of wonder and admiration for the awesome striking power of the British ships. Orders were placed in British yards, and, within a few years, Japan had a navy of her own, British built and with its officers trained by the Royal Navy. The Japanese Imperial Navy was therefore born of the Royal Navy and fashioned in its image. The traditions of tight discipline, efficiency and gentlemanly conduct, instilled in it by its mentors, lived on in the Imperial Navy for many years, enabling it to soundly beat the Russians in 1904 and to put up a most credible performance in the First World War.

The atrocities committed against Allied prisoners of war by the Japanese Army in World War II were legion and have been well documented. A thin defence for such absolute barbarism may be found in the ancient Bushido Code of the Samurai, which teaches that death, even by one's own hand, is infinitely preferable to dishonour. For the soldiers of Nippon to surrender and be taken into captivity by the enemy was the final indignity. They could not begin to comprehend how Allied troops were content to lay down their arms and surrender, when the odds were stacked too heavily against them. Such men, they reasoned, must be totally without honour and the kindliest thing that could be offered them was a quick death.

There was, perhaps, another contributory cause of the Japanese treatment of Allied prisoners. In the years leading up to World War II, an industrially growing Japan had begun to see herself as the champion of the millions of coloured people of Asia who lived under the heel of the imperialistic powers of the West. When, beginning with the fiasco of Pearl Harbor, Japanese forces easily inflicted one humiliating defeat after another on the former colonial masters of Asia, the myth of white supremacy was buried for ever. The urge to degrade, punish and exterminate the vanquished must have been very strong.

Whatever excuses are offered up for murder in its most brutal form – and that is what this was – it is hard to understand why Japanese sea-men turned their backs on the unwritten code of the sea. And it is even more strange that there are no recorded incidents of atrocities, committed at sea, against men of the fighting navies of the Allies. It seems that the relatively helpless merchant seamen were, for reasons unknown, singled out for special treatment. This book records the evil that befell some of them.

ONE

U nder the cover of darkness in the early hours of the morning of 10 May 1940, German Panzer divisions swarmed across the frontiers of Holland and rolled relentlessly over the flat green fields towards the North Sea. Putting an excess of faith in their natural defences, the Dutch planned to stop the enemy in his tracks by breaching the dykes of their vast network of canals. However, it took a lot more than a few feet of water to halt the German tanks, and the battle – if it could be called that – was over in four days. Rotterdam was raised to the ground by the Luftwaffe, and Queen Wilhelmina, her family and her Government, left for England.

At 11 am on the 15th the Dutch High Command surrendered to General von Bock, who led the lightning assault. For the time being, Holland in Europe was finished, but far across the seas to the east lay another Holland. In the fabulous Spice Islands of the East Indies, in Java and Sumatra, where sugar, tobacco, cocoa and tea grew in lush abundance, where coal, tin and oil were never far below ground, was a vast powerhouse with which the Dutch hoped to carry on the war from afar. Then came Pearl Harbor.

It is said that when, on 7 December 1941, Winston Churchill received news of the Japanese attack on Pearl Harbor, it was as though a great burden had been lifted from his shoulders. At that time Britain's resources were stretched to their utmost limits, while her reluctant ally, Russia, was in imminent danger of being overwhelmed by Hitler's steamrollering armies. Churchill considered that, with the might of the USA at last drawn into the fray, swift and ultimate victory was assured for the Allies. Great statesman though he was, he, in common with many others, seriously underestimated the power and ability of the Japanese war machine.

Three hundred and sixty Japanese carrier-borne aircraft took part in the raid on Pearl Harbor, and in less than half an hour, had wiped out four American battleships, one hundred and eighty-eight aircraft and nearly two and a half thousand men. The remainder of the US Pacific Fleet was crippled and another two thousand wounded lay under the pall of smoke covering the base. All this for the loss of just twenty-nine Japanese planes. And there was worse – much worse – to come.

Coincident with the attack on Pearl Harbor, Japanese troops landed in Thailand and Malaya, and began moving almost unopposed across the Kra Isthmus to the Indian Ocean. A few hours later, Hong Kong and US airfields in the Philipines received their first bombs, and for the British, perhaps, the unkindest cut of all.

On the evening of 8 December, the battleships Prince of Wales and Repulse, with four destroyers in company, sailed from Singapore and hurried northwards to attack Japanese forces landing on the east coast of Malaya. Forty-eight hours later, the 36,727-ton Prince of Wales, reputed to be the finest of her kind afloat, and her equally powerful consort, Repulse, were sent to the bottom by Japanese torpedo bombers, taking with them over a thousand men. In two bold forays the Japanese had, in two days, emasculated British and American naval power in the Far East, leaving no big guns afloat to oppose them anywhere in the Indian Ocean or Pacific.

It now seemed there was no way of stopping the rampaging Japanese, as with brilliant cut and thrust they changed the colour of the map. The Philipines and Borneo were invaded on the 10th, Penang fell on the 14th, Hong Kong surrendered on Christmas Day and Japanese troops entered Manila on New Year's Eve. In the Pacific the rays of the Rising Sun spread ever outwards, mopping up island after island and moving relentlessly southwards to New Guinea and Australia.

It is not surprising, then, that when the Dutch steamer Langkoeas left Sourabaya, Java on the evening of 1 January 1942, bound for Haifa with a full cargo of sugar, there was an air of some anxiety on board. Reports from the Pacific told of eight merchant ships already sunk by Japanese submarines; in the case of one of them, it was rumoured the survivors had been machine-gunned in the water.

The 7395-ton Langkoeas, flying the Netherlands flag and managed by the Rotterdam-Lloyd Company, was a new addition to the Dutch merchant fleet. Built in 1930 at the Bremer Vulkan yard on the River Weser for the crack Hamburg Amerika Line, she started life as the Stassfurt. On the outbreak of war in September 1939, fleeing from the Royal Navy, which at that time held sway in the Indian Ocean, she took refuge in the, then, neutral port of Tjilatjap, on the south coast of Java. There she lay for eight months, rusting and neglected, until, when Germany invaded Holland in May 1940, she was seized by the Royal Netherlands Navy and handed over to Rotterdam-Lloyd. They re-registered her in Tandjong-Priok and renamed her Langkoeas.

Having lain idle for so long, the Langkoeas was in a deplorable state when first taken over, and it was August 1941 before she was again ready for sea. Then, commanded by 49-year-old Captain Jan Kreumer, with Dutch officers, Chinese deck and engine-room ratings, and Javanese stewards – a total crew of 94, she made a successful maiden voyage to the Mediterranean, returning to Java via Colombo. It was on this voyage that the complexities and shortcomings of her engines became apparent. They, like so many German-built marine engines of her day, were the brainchildren of a designer who was either not aware, or had lost sight of, the strains imposed on the propulsion machinery of a commercially-oriented merchantman. In place of the reliable, virtually indestructible, triple-expansion, steam-reciprocating engine favoured by the vast majority of merchant steamers, she was driven by three steam turbines, geared to one drive shaft. The steam turbine, under the best of circumstances, is a delicate piece of machinery, finely balanced and requiring expert care and maintenance; three turbines driving one propellor shaft can constitute a nightmare. It was partly for this reason that the Langkoeas carried a total of 50 in her engine-room staff, a most disproportionate number for a 7000-ton merchant ship. However, it is unlikely she would have been thus endowed, had it not been for the fact that the Dutch Merchant Navy, having lost many of its ships, had a great excess of men. It was far better for them to be at sea than ashore. For the men it meant regular pay, and for the shipowners more, and better, maintenance in the engine-room, and, as the Government was footing the bill, this was a satisfactory arrangement all round.

One hour after sunset on the 2nd, the Langkoeas was 40 miles to the west of Bawean Island and making good progress towards Tandjong-Priok, where she was to make a brief call on the morning of the 4th. It was a warm, humid night, with the rumble of thunder bouncing off the distant hills of Java and the flash of lightning all around. There was menace in the air, but this did not disturb Fourth Engineer Jan de Mul when he emerged from the stifling heat of the engine-room. Leaning on the ship's side rail, he gazed out to sea and revelled in the cooling breeze that plucked at his sweat-soaked boiler suit. Emergency repairs to a circulating pump had kept him at work in the engine-room long after his watch was over. For a few moments de Mul's thoughts dwelled on the long voyage ahead and the dangers the ship might have to face, then, with a shrug of his shoulders, he turned his back on the sea and made for his cabin. He saw no virtue in worrying. More importantly, it was almost 7 pm, and he wanted nothing more than to snatch a few hours sleep before taking up his watch again at midnight. But first he needed to wash off the grime and sweat of the engine-room under a cool shower.

On the bridge of the Dutch ship, Chief Officer C.J. van de Boom was also nearing the end of his day's work, and, like de Mul, had thoughts of a well-earned rest to come. Apart from keeping the 4 to 8 watch on the bridge morning and evening, as chief officer, van de Boom was responsible for the care and maintenance of the deck. This, and a certain amount of paper work, occupied the hours between watches, so that his working day often stretched, with only short breaks for meals, from four in the morning to eight at night. But, fatigued though he might be, van de Boom did not relax his vigilance, sweeping the dark horizon from time to time with his binoculars. It may have been the oppressive weather, or it may have been because he was acutely aware that war had finally come to the Java Sea, but van de Boom was uneasy. And, although he did not know it, he had good cause to be. Hidden in the darkness to starboard, a feather of white phosphorescence glided through the oily swells. The Japanese submarine I-58 had arrived in the Java Sea.

Commanded by Lieutenant-Commander S. Kitamura, I-58 was one of the Japanese Navy's older submarines, one of a class of fifteen boats built in the early 1930s. She was of 1635 tons displacement and armed with 16 torpedoes, a 4.7-inch deck gun and several light machine-guns. Her surface range was 10,000 miles at 10 knots, she had a top surface speed of 20 knots and a submerged speed of 8 knots. Unlike her British and American counterparts, she carried no radar, was slow to submerge and clumsy to handle. In compensation for her shortcomings, she was crewed by 89 volunteers, all trained to perfection at Japan's submarine school at Yokosuka in Tokyo Bay.

When, in early November 1941, the Japanese Government made the secret decision to attack America, I-58, accompanied by five other boats of the 4th Squadron, to which she belonged, slipped silently out of her base and disappeared into the wide reaches of the Pacific Ocean. War had come soon enough, but with it bitter disappointment for Lieutenant Commander Kitamura. Weeks of patrolling in the Pacific yielded nothing but an empty horizon and dreary monotony. His crew, unblooded but eager, were now showing signs of restlessness and he was running short on fuel and provisions. The order to move south into the Java Sea, where it was said rich pickings were to be had, helped to ease the tension, but Kitamura knew the time would soon come when he would be forced to return to base to replenish his dwindling resources. Was he to suffer the terrible ignominy of returning without so much as an enemy fishing boat to his credit? The thought of the loss of face involved was too awful to contemplate.

The change of watch came and went in the Langkoeas, while in the cramped conning tower of I-58, Kitamura continued to sweep the horizon with his night glasses, cursing the passing rainstorms which, from time to time, blotted out his vision. Grudgingly, he gave thanks for the cool night breeze. The sea temperature was in excess of 30 Centigrade and he appreciated that below him in the hull of the boat his men were suffering, the damp heat adding to their frustration. There was not a man among them, Kitamura mused, who would not give his eye teeth to be back in Japan. There, the typhoon season was over and the wind would be blowing fresh and steady from the north-west, sending clouds, like playful balls of cotton wool, scudding across a flawless blue sky. The image of Mount Fuji, capped with pristine snow, was filling his mind's eye when, suddenly, he jerked erect. Ahead and to port, briefly illuminated by a flash of lightning, he had seen the low outline of a heavily laden ship. Kitamura called for diving stations.

Jan de Mul, exhausted by his long slog in the heat of the engine-room, had fallen asleep on his settee, unshowered and still in his oil and sweat-stained boilersuit. He awoke, somewhat bemused, to the crash of the exploding torpedo, the cabin lights were still on, and when he looked at his watch, saw he had been asleep for only just over an hour. Then the Langkoeas gave a lurch to starboard, the lights went out and the room was suddenly filled with the acrid stench of burning cordite. De Mul, his mind now alert, rolled off the settee, snatched up his lifejacket and "panic bag" containing his personal papers, a few valuables and a tin of cigarettes, and left the cabin in a hurry.

He found the alleyway in complete darkness and filled with smoke and fumes. The engineers' accommodation was directly over the engine-room and it was clear to de Mul, as he groped his way towards the after door leading to the deck, that the torpedo had struck the machinery space, thereby ripping open the Langkoeas's most vulnerable compartment. His assessment was confirmed when he met other engineers seeking to escape. The word was that twelve men, on watch below, had been killed.

On the open deck it appeared to be even darker, as though the perpertrators of this evil deed had drawn a black curtain around the scene to hide the carnage from the eyes of the outside world. The cry of "Abandon ship!" had gone up and hysterical Chinese and Javanese crewmen ran, like headless chickens, in all directions. The Langkoeas lurched upright and began to settle by the stern. De Mul knew it was time to make for the boat deck.

The Langkoeas carried four lifeboats, de Mul's designated station being at the after, starboard boat. By the time he reached his station, his eyes had adjusted to the darkness and it was plain he would have to look elsewhere for salvation. His boat had been reduced to a pile of matchwood by the explosion.

Crossing quickly to the port side of the deck, de Mul found a place in the after lifeboat, which was already overcrowded and on the point of being lowered. Disaster struck even as he climbed over the gunwale. The Chinese seamen, detailed to lower the boat and fearful that they might be left behind, cast off too many turns of the rope falls, lost control, and the heavily laden boat fell like a stone to the water below.

Crowded with struggling humanity, the wooden lifeboat weighed in the region of three tons, and, falling from a height of some twenty feet, hit the water with such force that it was completely submerged. Most of the boat's occupants were thrown out, and when it came to the surface again, Jan de Mul, who had had the good sense to find a firm handhold, was one of only half a dozen remaining men.

The clouds chose that moment to draw apart, allowing a newly risen moon to shed its light on the scene, and with it came new heart for de Mul and his shocked and half-drowned companions. Urged on by the engineer, they began to bail out the waterlogged boat, using their shoes; the bailers, along with most of the other loose gear in the boat, having been washed over the side. It was a task bordering on the impossible, but it took their minds off the predicament they were in.

In the light of the moon the situation around them became clearer and de Mul was delighted to see the Langkoeas's motor lifeboat, in charge of Captain Kreumer, was heading towards them with another boat in tow. But his joy turned to horror when he saw the dark silhouette of the submarine, 200 metres off the other boats, and bearing down on them at speed. For some unexplained reason – perhaps because they were seeing the submarine from a different angle – most of the men in those boats thought that rescue had come and were standing on the thwarts cheering their good luck.

Thigh-deep in the tepid water of their flooded boat, de Mul and the others were silent witnesses to the carnage that followed. They heard the crackle of machine-gun fire, tracers arced through the air and the cheering occupants of the other boats were toppled like coconuts at a fairground. Men screamed, first in disbelief, then in agony as they bled and died. The firing continued for a long time, until the two lifeboats, riddled from gunwale to keel, had sunk, leaving the sea covered with lifeless bodies. Then there was silence.

Perhaps, if de Mul and those with him had possessed the presence of mind to jump overboard, or at least crouch down in the boat, they might have escaped the attention of I-58. Unfortunately, the terrible massacre they had witnessed held them transfixed, still clutching the shoes they had been using in lieu of bailers. The submarine approached to within 100 metres of the boat and then its guns opened up again.

It was only when the man standing alongside him gave a startled grunt and fell back clutching his chest that de Mul's brain began to function sensibly. He threw himself over the side and kicked out, desperate to get away from the sinking boat that had, in its turn, become an executioner's platform.

When he came to the surface, de Mul found himself only centimetres off the rust-streaked hull of the submarine as it slid past him. Pure instinct prompted him to reach out for one of the projecting hydroplanes and he was dragged unceremoniously through the water. Confused and frightened, the thought of releasing his hold did not occur to him, and, when a few minutes later, I-58 came to a halt, hands reached down and dragged him onto the casing like a drowned rat.

De Mul was soon in no doubt as to the identity of his captors. Falsetto voices jabbered at him, a revolver was jammed into the pit of his stomach and he caught the glint of an unsheathed sword. They were small men, dressed in khaki, with shapeless peaked caps; they could only be Japanese. Seized with a sudden panic, he tried to break away, but the sword slashed at his left leg and he felt excrutiating pain. Like an errant schoolboy, he was pushed, slapped and bundled towards the foot of the conning tower, where two other crew members of the Langkoeas, a Chinese deck rating and a Javanese steward, stood shivering in fear.

The commander of the submarine now appeared and began to interrogate de Mul in pidgin English. Each question was accompanied by a threat of punishment if not answered. Kitamura demanded to know the name of the ship he had sunk, the nature of her cargo, her loading port and destination. De Mul was filled with loathing for this man who had so ruthlessly slaughtered his shipmates, but, surrounded by armed men and with blood dripping from the wound in his leg, he was hardly in a position to withhold information. In any case, he reasoned, the ship had gone, so his answers could do no more damage. It was only when Kitamura began to question him about secret codes and signals that he realised the Japanese commander had mistaken him for either the master or a senior deck officer of the Langkoeas. He hastened to explain that he was a mere junior engineer and had no knowledge of such things. At this Kitamura flew into a fit of rage, spat out the words, "You go home, then!" and stormed off. As he left, the other Japanese closed on de Mul, punching and kicking him, and finally hurled him bodily back into the sea from whence he had come. The Chinese sailor and the Javanese steward followed him a few minutes later.

Fortunately for the three men, they were still wearing their lifejackets, and, in spite of the ordeal they had been through, they had the good sense to paddle clear of the submarine. They watched silently and with mixed feelings as the water churned up around I-58's propellors and, with her exhausts roaring, she disappeared into the night.

Jan de Mul's immediate concern was to locate and maintain contact with the others, but he feared they were all that remained of the Langkoeas's crew. He hoped that when daylight came they might be able to find a life raft or some wreckage to cling to, but his calls went unanswered and, with the swells running high, he could see no more than a few feet around him. For the rest of the night he drifted alone, in a dream-like state, always conscious of his injured leg and the blood seeping from the wound. In his tortured imagination, the dark waters around him were populated with silent, stalking sharks, waiting for the opportune moment to strike.

When dawn broke at last, the young engineer's nerves were at breaking point. As the sun rose and warmed him, he experienced a brief surge of optimism. He had survived a terrifying ordeal at the hands of the Japanese, followed by a night of fear. From now on, he reasoned desperately, things must improve, yet the hopelessness of his position left him with a sinking feeling, in a stomach already contracting through lack of food. Rising and falling on the oily swells, he was alone with nothing to support him but a lifejacket with a limited life. He had no idea how far off the land he was, nor in which direction it lay. It seemed that his escape from the Japanese bullets had condemned him to die a lingering and lonely death.

The sun rose higher in the sky and its comforting warmth turned to a searing furnace, bringing on a raging thirst that fortunately diverted de Mul's mind away from the problem of survival. He drifted in a daze, dreaming of tumbling waterfalls of clear, sparkling water, hearing the clink of ice in long, frosted glasses until the waves began to slap at his face, arousing him sufficiently to realise he was gradually sinking lower in the water. The kapok filling of his lifejacket had become saturated and was dragging him down. He looked up at the sun, now almost overhead, and tried to remember for how long a lifejacket was designed to keep a man afloat. Was it twenty-four or forty-eight hours? The answer was irrelevant, for by mid-afternoon he was forced to abandon the sodden jacket. Fortunately, he was a powerful swimmer and had no difficulty in staying afloat. The loss of his support, in fact, acted as a stimulus, encouraging him to strike out and explore his immediate surroundings. Very shortly he came across a damaged life raft.

Hauling himself on board the raft with difficulty, for his injured leg was still painful, de Mul lay face down on the broken boards and gave thanks that his run of bad luck had at last changed. The raft had been severely shot up by the Japanese, but its buoyancy tanks had not been pierced. It would keep him afloat indefinitely. He soon discovered, however, there was no food or water on board, yet such was his initial relief at finding the raft, he gave this little thought. During the next two hours he sighted and rescued from the sea the Chinese sailor Lam Dai and the Javanese steward Lajar. Both these men had been wearing so-called "old fashioned" cork lifejackets, which, ironically, had kept them afloat much longer than de Mul's modern kapok type.

Incredibly, a few hours later Dame Fortune smiled again. De Mul had stood up on the raft to take a look around, when to his great relief he saw a small boat, apparently empty, rising and falling on the swell about a quarter of a mile off. Telling the others to remain where they were, he dived overboard and swam with long, powerful strokes towards the boat. This he found to be the Langkoeas's work-boat, a stout 12-footer used for painting round the ship. Normally stowed on the after deck and only lightly secured, the boat must have floated off when the ship sank. De Mul hoisted himself over the gunwale and was little surprised to find the boat holed by bullets and partly filled with water. As it was not a lifeboat in the true sense of the word, it contained no provisions or fresh water, but it did have two oars, a mast and a small sail. Using one of the oars, de Mul sculled the boat back to the raft and picked up his fellow survivors. By nightfall the three men had stopped the leaks, bailed the boat dry, and were ready to make a bid for land.

The course they took was pre-determined, for the clumsy boat with its scrap of sail would only run before the wind, which was from the west – so it was to the east they went. De Mul had a vague notion that Bawean Island, 150 miles north of Sourabaya, lay in that direction, although he had no idea of the distance involved.

For the next four days, scorched by the blazing sun during the day and shivering in the torrential rains that came at night, the three survivors sailed eastwards at a snail's pace. It was only the nightly rainfall that kept them alive, for they were thus able to quench their thirst, but their bellies were empty, and they became weaker and weaker, oblivious to the passing days.

It may have been by divine intervention or just sheer luck that they ran ashore on the island of Bawean on 7 January. A local fisherman found them lying in the bottom of their boat, suffering from severe sunburn and so weak that they were unable to crawl ashore. The fisherman summoned assistance and the survivors were soon jolting along a dirt-track road in an ancient motor car to the island's capital, Sangkapoera. From there a Catalina flew them to Batavia, where they were admitted to the local hospital.

Out of a total crew of 94, Jan de Mul, Lam Dai and Lajar were the only survivors of the sinking of the Langkoeas. Twelve had died in the engine-room when the torpedo struck, 79 others perished in that frenzy of killing on the night of 2 January 1942, victims, presumably, of the loathsome code of Bushido. It is unlikely that Captain Jan Kreumer and his men subscribed to this "death before dishonour"

21

concept. In any case, they were given no choice by the men who came out of the darkness with guns.

Jan de Mul recovered quickly from his ordeal, and, towards the end of February, anxious to return to sea, was appointed to sail in the steamer Boero, bound for Australia. Providentially, he fell ill before he could join her and was re-admitted to hospital. On 25 February the Boero was torpedoed and sunk in the Sunda Strait, again by I-58. This time Kitamura left no survivors to tell the tale of his infamy.

De Mul was still in hospital when Java was overrun by the Japanese in the first week in March. He escaped to join a resistance group set up on the island but was later captured by the Japanese, endured further horrors in a prison camp, and was officially listed as dead in 1943. Like a phoenix rising out of the ashes, he reappeared at the end of the war, very much alive, although badly scarred physically and mentally. Jan de Mul was a man the Japanese could not kill.

I-58 torpedoed, but failed to sink, the British tanker British Judge in the Sunda Strait on 28 February 1942, thereafter she disappeared from view, presumably withdrawn from service or accidentally lost in some obscure corner of the Pacific. Lieutenant Commander Kitamura showed up briefly in October 1942 in command of I-27, but then also disappeared. He may have survived the war, but he was certainly never brought to trial for the atrocities he committed.

TWO

The relentless Japanese war machine gathered momentum. On 15 February 1942, in one of the most ignominious defeats in recent history, 85,000 British troops laid down their arms and that impregnable bastion of the Empire, Singapore, along with the whole of the Malaysian peninsular, fell into Japanese hands. Bali surrendered on the 18th, and Timor a few days later. Northern Australia was now only one hour's flying time for Japanese bombers. But it was aircraft of Admiral Nagumo's fast carrier group, which had moved into the Timor Sea, that delivered the first blow by attacking Darwin on the 19th.

Darwin, Australia's only port in the far north, was at that time packed with Allied ships, mostly merchantmen, who were caught unawares when 242 Japanese bombers swooped in from the sea. The port had very little in the way of anti-aircraft defences and it was left to the ships to fight back as best they could with their own guns, but these were no match for the bombers, and the harbour and town were reduced to smoking ruins. When they had exhausted their bombs, the

Japanese pilots completed their mission by machine-gunning lifeboats and helpless survivors struggling in the water. At the end of the day, eight ships had been sunk and nine others severely damaged; 170 Allied seamen lay dead and more than 300 injured. It was a day of horror Darwin would never forget. Second Officer Pierre Payne, who was serving aboard the tanker British Motorist, describes the attack on his ship:

"They came in at high level at first and dropped three salvoes of twelve bombs. These shattered the side of the ship. After that they just kept coming. I was on the 12-pounder aft by the funnel and over the engine-room. Every time they came around we aimed and fired. This seemed to put them off. Unfortunately, one came out of the sun astern and dropped a bomb that hit the bridge. The Captain was thrown onto the deck and the Second Radio Officer killed. She was on fire amidships and took another bomb. We had Indian crew who were panicking, and eventually we had to abandon ship. The Chief Officer stayed on the ship to look after the Captain, who had a leg blown off. I managed to get a boat away and decided to make for the shore rather than the jetty, which was fortunate. A ship alongside the jetty laden with depth charges blew up. But that was war. What we didn't like was when they turned their attention to the Australian hospital ship, which was clearly marked – painted with white crosses. They bombed and machine-gunned her. That was not war – that was sheer murder."

For Pierre Payne this was a grim introduction to Japanese brutality. He was to see much more of it, and at very close quarters, before the war was over.

And now the last days of Holland's great empire in the East were drawing near. On 26 February, an invasion force under Admiral Sokichi, consisting of 97 troop transports, protected by 14 destroyers,

2 light cruisers and 2 heavy cruisers, appeared in the Java Sea. They were met on the 27th by a hastily assembled Allied fleet – a hotch-potch of British, Dutch, American and Australian warships under the Dutch Rear-Admiral Doorman. The Allied ships were outnumbered, outgunned and running short of fuel, but, over the next two days they fought a series of gallant actions, during which all but four of them were sunk. Admiral Doorman, who at all times led from the front, went down with his ship the cruiser De Ruyter. The island of Java fell on 7 March, and two days later, the whole of the Dutch East Indies was in Japanese hands.

While the Battle of the Java Sea was in progress, the Dutch tanker Augustina slipped out of Tandjong Priok, on Java's north-west coast, hoping to escape to Australia. On 1 March, she was 300 miles south of Christmas Island when the Japanese destroyer Harukaze, one of the victors of the Java Sea, caught up with her. The Augustina's crew of 30, abandoned ship in two lifeboats, having first set scuttling charges in the bottom of their ship. Under the circumstances, these men had done all that could have been asked of them; they then expected the Japanese to extend to them the usual courtesy of the sea by treating them as survivors. Their innocence cost them dearly. The Harukaze closed in on the boats and opened fire with her machine-guns. Only one man survived.

In early April, Nagumo's ships moved into the Indian Ocean, and at 08.00 on Easter Sunday, 5 April, 127 carrier-borne aircraft raided Colombo, causing major damage to the port. Later in the day, to the south-west of Ceylon, the British cruisers Dorsetshire and Cornwall were bombed and sunk with the loss of 424 lives. Early next morning, two heavy cruisers and a destroyer of Nagumo's force intercepted an unescorted British convoy in the Bay of Bengal, and in under two hours sent 11 ships to the bottom. On the 9th, Japanese planes attacked the naval base at Trincomalee, sinking HMS Hermes, one of only three British aircraft carriers remaining in Eastern Waters. The destroyer Vampire and the corvette Hollyhock were also lost in this raid.

Not surprisingly, the Admiralty now decided to move the remainder of Admiral Somerville's Eastern Fleet from Trincomalee to the East African port of Mombasa, where it was hoped it could be reorgansied and strengthened to match Nagumo's force. The Indian Ocean then became an Axis lake, through which all Allied shipping passed at its peril. During the first ten days of April, Japanese submarines, roaming unmolested, sank 145,000 tons of Allied merchant shipping. In early May, the armed merchant cruisers Hokoku Maru and Aikoku Maru left their base at Singapore to join the fray.

Built in 1940 at the Tama Shipyard in Osaka for Osaka Shosen Kaisha, the Hokoku Maru and Aikoku Maru were sister ships of 10,500 tons gross, having twin-screws powered by two 12-cylinder diesel engines. They were aristocratic, 18-knot ships, owned by a prestigious cargo liner company, and it was inevitable that when war came they were both drafted into the Japanese Imperial Navy. Painted grey overall and armed with six 6-inch guns, two torpedo tubes, an array of anti-aircraft guns, and two catapult spotter planes, the raiders presented a formidible threat to Allied shipping.

Immediately after Pearl Harbor, the Hokoku Maru, commanded by Commander Hirishi Imatsato, and the Aikoku Maru with Commander Tamatso Oishi in command, moved into the South Pacific and began operations against US merchant ships. Their initial performance was not impressive; in a cruise lasting five weeks they sank only two ships. The raiders then returned to Japan and were not seen again until they appeared in the Indian Ocean acting as supply ships to the 8th Submarine Flotilla under Vice-Admiral Ishizaki. On 9 May, the two ships, acting in consort, captured the 7987-ton Dutch tanker Genota, on passage from Australia to the Persian Gulf. A prize crew was put on board the tanker and she was taken to Singapore. The Imperial Navy's investment in the two ex-merchantmen was beginning to show returns. However, valuable targets like the Genota had become scarce in the upper reaches of the Indian Ocean and Admiral Ishizaki decided to take his force south of Madagascar, where Allied ships, bound to and from India via the Cape of Good Hope, were to be found passing in considerable numbers.

At dawn on 5 June the 6757-ton British cargo/passenger liner Elysia was in the southern approaches to the Mozambique Channel and heading north to pass between Madgascar and the African mainland. The weather was fine, with few clouds and a light north-westerly wind, a state of affairs that would soon change. In a day or two, Chief Officer Colqhoun reflected as he took his morning star sights, they would soon run into the South-West Monsoon. Low, scudding cloud, driving rain and rough seas would then greet every dawn, and render his sextant temporarily redundant.

The 34-year-old Elysia, owned by the Anchor Line of Glasgow, a veteran of the First World War, would have been pensioned off if it had not been for the outbreak of hostilities in 1939. She had already survived a brush with a Fokker-Wulf, and, despite her advanced age, continued to play a useful role in keeping open the sea lanes to Britain. Concurrent with the arrival of the Japanese Fleet in the Indian Ocean, the Elysia left the Firth of Clyde, bound for Bombay, carrying, in her holds, the vehicles of a motorised battalion of the King's Royal Rifles, and, on deck, crates of fighter aircraft for the RAF. In her midships accommodation she carried 17 passengers, a mixture of civilians and servicemen, all with a part to play in the war in the East. She was commanded by Captain Morrison, who had distinguished himself in action during the attack on the Jervis Bay convoy by the Admiral Scheer in the winter of 1940, and was manned by British officers and Indian ratings.

The Elysia's outward passage to Cape Town passed without incident. She left Table Bay on 1 June and, sailing unescorted at a speed of 12 knots, was expected to reach Bombay on or about the 16th of the month.

At 07.30 on the 5th, Chief Officer Colqhoun was nearing the end of his watch and looking forward to a hearty breakfast of bacon and eggs, when he sighted two unidentified ships bearing down on the Elysia from the north-east. He immediately called Captain Morrison to the bridge.

Morrison examined the approaching ships through his binoculars, noting their high midships superstructure, raked bows and array of cargo derricks. They were both, he estimated, about 10,000 tons gross and had a distinctive "eastern" look to them. In more peaceful days, he would have taken them for Japanese cargo/passenger vessels bound for the Cape, but times being what they were, Morrison was suspicious. The determination and speed with which the two ships continued to head for the Elysia soon convinced him the newcomers were up to no good, and he was not inclined to hang about awaiting their intentions. He rang for emergency full speed and swung the Elysia through 180 degrees, presenting her stern to the strangers.

The Hokoku Maru and Aikoku Maru, steaming in line astern, were not about to let their first likely prey, in almost a month, escape so easily. A signal lamp flashed urgently from the leading ship demanding that the Elysia heave-to.

Morrison's answer was to send his gun's crew aft to man the liner's single 4.7-inch. By this time, the ship, with her boiler safety valves screwed down tight, had worked up to 13œ knots. She was vibrating so fiercely it seemed likely that every rivet in her solid, Clyde-built hull must pop. But her Japanese pursuers – they had now been clearly identified as such – were gaining ground, and soon bright stabs of flame reached out from their forecastles. The shells began to burst around the fleeing Elysia.

A lesser man than Morrison would now have given up, for the odds against him were very great. But he had been war-hardened in the Battle of the Atlantic, and although his ship was slow and poorly armed, Morrison meant to make a fight of it. He first ordered the Elysia's wireless operator to send out the RRR signal, indicating to all stations that she was under attack by a surface raider. He then passed the word aft for the gun's crew to open fire on the Japanese.

In hindsight, it was perhaps fortunate Captain Morrison had on the bridge with him Chief Officer Colqhoun and Second Officer Ure, who counselled against taking on the two heavily armed Japanese ships. Not only was the Elysia's 4.7-inch of First World War vintage, but she had only 12 rounds of ammunition in her locker. Clearly the fight would be hopelessly one-sided and could only end in tragedy. Morrison was persuaded to hold his fire, but was still determined to escape, if at all possible. He refused to slow down.

The Japanese gunners had now found the range, and broadsides were bracketing the Elysia every few minutes. Morrison ordered smoke floats to be dropped over the stern and began a nerve-wracking evasive zig-zag, steering towards each flurry of bursting shells, working on the principle that lightning never strikes twice in the same place.

For over an hour, under the cover of her smoke screen, and through the consummate skill and coolness of her captain, the Elysia fled for her life. Then her supply of smoke floats ran out and she was left completely exposed to the heavy guns of the raiders, who had closed the range considerably. Shells, high-explosive and shrapnel, rained down on the helpless merchant ship, smashing into her accommodation and bridge.

It was a bitter pill for Morrison to swallow, but he knew the situation was hopeless and that he must now think of saving his crew. Having stopped the engine, he hoisted the international code signal indicating he was abandoning ship, and gave the order to lower the lifeboats.

By the grace of God and Morrison's expertise, not a man had been lost during the prolonged shelling. There was some panic amongst the Indian crew when abandoning ship, but all the Elysia's passengers and crew got away in the boats. The success of the operation was largely due to the fact that the Japanese ships held their fire while the boats were being lowered.

Once the boats were clear of the ship, the raiders continued their shelling, but the Elysia was a tough old ship and stubbornly refused to sink. The guns fell silent once again and the Hokoku Maru launched her seaplane, which dropped four bombs on the Elysia, scoring only one hit, also with little effect. The guns opened up again, but it was not until the raiders closed in and torpedoed the liner that she began to settle by the stern.

The Elysia's survivors feared, as they watched the destruction of their ship from the boats, that the Japanese might now turn their wrath on them, for it was rumoured that they were in the habit of killing survivors. By refusing to stop and then running away, they had offered provocation enough, but to their great relief, the raiders ignored them and steamed off over the horizon. Fifteen hours later, Morrison, his passengers and crew, were rescued, unharmed, by the British hospital ship Dorsetshire, which had arrived in answer to the Elysia's distress calls. Although when last seen the Elysia appeared to be on the point of sinking, she was reported to have remained afloat for another four days before taking her final plunge.

There can be no argument that during the prolonged action the Hokoku Maru and Aikoku Maru conducted themselves in the best traditions of war at sea, as laid down by the Royal Navy. When the Elysia refused to heave-to in response to their signals, they were perfectly justified in opening fire. They also acted with considerable compassion by holding their fire while Morrison abandoned ship. It had been, in all, a most gentlemanly action, but was destined to be one of the few examples of its kind involving the Japanese Imperial Navy in the Second World War.

The Hokoku Maru and Aikoku Maru now moved deeper into the Indian Ocean, and after more than a month of searching those lonely waters, they sank the 7113-ton British motor vessel Hauraki 780 miles south-east of Diego Garcia. A week later, on 19 July, the raiders put into Penang for a refit. Again, they had steamed many thousands of miles for very little reward; two ships sunk and one captured would earn Imatsato and Oishi no medals. The five 1st class submarines of the 8th Flotilla, on the other hand, had achieved spectacular success, sinking in June and July no less than 22 Allied merchant ships of 103,487 tons. Vice Admiral Ishizaki had good reason to be proud of his submariners.

THREE

When Iran's Shah Riza Khan was eased into comfortable exile in South Africa in the winter of 1941, he left behind him a country in turmoil. Not least amongst the problems facing the British occupation forces, who had moved in to forestall a German take-over of the oil fields, was a sudden and acute shortage of food. Before leaving the country, the wily old Shah had secretly disposed of Iran's entire stock of grain, shipping this through Turkey to Germany, where his real loyalty lay. Within weeks, Iran was on the verge of starvation and the responsibility for feeding its 15 million-plus populace fell squarely on the already overburdened shoulders of the British Government.

Conveniently, a solution was to hand. Six thousand miles to the south, on Australia's southern coastal belt, the granaries were overflowing. However, the dry-cargo ships required to carry the grain to Iran were in short supply, being mainly engaged in shipping more warlike cargoes. It was for this reason the Dutch tanker Ondina found herself unexpectedly involved in the grain trade.

Built in 1939 at Amsterdam for the Royal Dutch Shell Company, the Ondina's maiden voyage had taken her across the Atlantic to load lubricating oils for the UK. She then spent some time trading in the Caribbean, and when Holland fell in May 1940, she was taken under the wing of the British Ministry of War Transport and returned to the cross-Atlantic run. Although continuing to fly the Dutch flag, she was from then on part of Britain's merchant fleet. Following Pearl Harbor, she was despatched to the Indian Ocean, where her services were needed to help keep the oil flowing from the Persian Gulf to Australia. It had been a simple matter of expediency for the Ondina to carry, on her ballast passages to the Gulf, as much bagged grain as could be conveniently loaded. This was stowed in her forward tanks and usually amounted to about 250 tons.

When, at the end of October 1942, Captain Willem Horsman joined the Ondina she was at a lay-by berth in Fremantle, Western Australia, having completed discharge of a cargo of petroleum products from Abadan. Shore labour was already at work washing out her two forward tanks preparatory to loading the customary parcel of grain for Iran. At first sight, Horsman, a 33-year-old Amsterdamer newly promoted to command, was well pleased with his ship.

The Ondina, a motor vessel of 6341 tons gross, was soundly built, and, in the best traditions of the Dutch Merchant Navy, in an excellent state of repair and cleanliness. She carried a total crew of 56, made up of 12 Dutch officers, 35 Chinese ratings and 9 DEMS gunners. Her six-cylinder Werkspoor diesel engine gave a top speed of 12 knots and she behaved well in bad weather. For ten months she had been employed on the shuttle service between Abadan and Australian ports, bringing in a cargo of 9000 tons of oil every two months. Each round voyage of 11,000 miles commenced and ended in Fremantle, which, quite naturally, became her adopted home port. The weather in the Indian Ocean being a great improvement on the habitually stormy

Atlantic, and the hospitality of the Australian people always without equal, it was not surprising the Ondina's crew were more than satisfied with their lot. In all respects, then, the Ondina was a well-found and happy ship.

It had been the custom for the Ondina to sail unescorted to and from the Gulf, however, when Willem Horsman joined her in Fremantle, he found he was to have company on his first voyage in command. The 650-ton Royal Indian Navy minesweeper Bengal, recently completed in an Australian shipyard was to sail with the Ondina as far as Diego Garcia. The 16-knot minesweeper, bound for Colombo, was unable to carry sufficient fuel for the 3000-mile passage to Diego Garcia, hence she was to accompany the Ondina, which would have on board an extra 150 tons of fuel oil to top up the Navy ship's tanks. Obviously, the Admiralty was also of the opinion that the two ships could offer mutual protection to each other on the long ocean passage. The Bengal, Horsman had been informed, was armed with a 4-inch gun, a quick-firing Bofors, two 20 mm Oerlikons and several light machine-guns. She would certainly make a formidible opponent for any enemy submarine or aircraft they chanced to meet on the way.

The Ondina's own defensive armament consisted of a 4-inch anti-submarine gun, one twin-Marlin and six Lewis machine-guns. The ship's gunnery officer was Second Officer Bartele Bakker, who had under his command the nine DEMS gunners; a somewhat mixed bunch. Led by 24-year-old Able Seaman Gunlayer Herbert Hammond of the Royal Australian Naval Reserve, were Able Seaman Raymond Bayliss, Able Seaman William Lukis, Able Seaman Henry Brooklyn and Able Seaman Henry Boyce of the Royal Navy, Bombardier William Nicoll, Lance-Bombardier William Kidd, Gunner Frank Ryan, all of the Royal Artillery's Maritime Regiment, and Able Seaman Gunner Muus Visser of the Dutch Merchant Navy. They were a good team, disciplined and, despite their diverse backgrounds, able to work easily together. Their main piece of armament, the 4-inch mounted on the Ondina's after deck, was an up-to-date model in excellent condition.

It seemed most unlikely that the Dutch tanker's gunners would be put to the test on the voyage. There were rumours that the German surface raider Michel had entered the Indian Ocean from the South Atlantic, but she would not be expected to venture much to the east of Madagascar. Similarly, it was apparent that U-boats successfully operating off the Cape and Durban had little incentive to move further afield. As for the Japanese, although they were in control of the whole of the East Indies, from Timor to the Andamans, there had been very few reports that they were active in the southern part of the Indian Ocean. Such was the current appraisal of the man-made dangers of the voyage. As for the weather, the season promised blue skies and relatively calm seas. With the support and company of HMIS Bengal, Horsman looked forward to a pleasant run to the north.

Odina at Rotterdam, June 1945

With 240 tons of grain stowed in her Nos 1 and 2 cargo tanks and with all other tanks empty, except for the Bengal's fuel oil, the Ondina slipped her moorings at Fremantle early on the morning of 5 November. A last minute addition to her complement, Able Seaman Richard Henry, Royal Australian Navy, stood on her after deck staring disconsolately at the disappearing shore. Henry, a member of the crew of HMIS Bengal hoped his stay in the tanker would be brief. Due to a miscalculation made by the administration ashore, he had missed his ship when returning from leave and was a passenger in the Ondina until he could be transferred to the Bengal at sea.

On the tanker's forecastle head, as she passed through the break-waters and lifted to the first of the Indian Ocean swells, Chief Officer Maarten Rehwinkel paced impatiently as the carpenter secured the anchors. Rehwinkel had a full programme of work planned for his 16-man Chinese deck crew and was anxious to make a start. Following ten months hard running on the Abadan-Australia shuttle the Ondina was badly in need of a coat of paint, and the fair weather passage ahead presented the ideal opportunity.

In his tiny wireless cabin below the bridge, Radio Officer R.W. van Gelderen was making a routine check of his equipment. Unlike in most Allied merchant ships, which carried three wireless operators and kept a listening watch around the clock, at sea, van Gelderen was alone on the Ondina. His orders were to cover only the hours 06.00 to 22.00, working two hours on and two hours off. In times of peace, with much of the watch spent chatting to other ships and shore sta-tions, the hours passed quickly, but things were different in wartime. Radio silence was imperative and the long watches were often spent listening to nothing more interesting than atmospheric crackles. Only in a case of dire emergency was van Gelderen authorised to switch on his transmitter and reach for the morse key. For him much of the voyage would be boring.

On the Ondina's bridge, Second Officer Bartele Bakker and Third Officer C.C. Hederick stood in the starboard wing and and took a last long look at the receding land. For them, as for the majority of the tanker's crew, the leaving of Australia's shores was always tinged with regret, the wide open spaces, the temperate climate, and the warm, outgoing people had become very much a part of their lives in exile. They would be counting the days until their return.

In the wheelhouse, Willem Horsman's mind was on more immediate matters. Stroking his chin thoughtfully, he was examining the low silhouette of the Ondina's passage companion to Diego Garcia. The Bengal looked far too small and vulnerable to attempt the long ocean voyage. He hoped she would not prove to be a liability.

Far out to sea, Acting Lieutenant Commander William Wilson, Royal Indian Naval Volunteer Reserve, surveyed the approaching tanker from his tiny open bridge with an equal lack of enthusiasm. The huge ship – huge in comparison with the Bengal's 650 tons – looked painfully slow and awkward. She had declared her speed as 12 knots, but Wilson was well aware that masters of merchant ships had a habit of overstating the capabilities of their commands – a matter of pride, he suspected. However, Wilson took some comfort from the knowledge that the Dutchman carried a 4-inch gun, manned, it was claimed, by a first class DEMS crew. It was not that Wilson lacked confidence in the Bengal and her predominantly Indian crew of 74, but she had come to sea ill-armed for any fight she might become involved in. The original specification called for a 4-inch, a Bofors, two Oerlikons and a number of light machine-guns, but for reasons not disclosed to Wilson, the complete package had gone missing in transit somewhere in Australia. In its place had been substituted a single 12-pounder and 40 rounds of ammunition, rendering the Bengal a tiger with most of its teeth missing.

Wilson would have been even more troubled had he been able to see beyond the far horizon. As the Bengal idled off Fremantle awaiting her consort, 2400 miles to the north, the Hokoku Maru and Aikoku Maru were leaving Penang. Having taken advantage of the excellent facilities of the ex-Royal Naval dockyard in the port, the Japanese AMCs were returning to the Indian Ocean intent on improving their dismal records. The two heavily armed, 18-knot ships were to operate without the support of submarines and, as before, were commanded by Commander Hirishi Imatsato and Commander Tamatso Oishi. Being the senior officer, Imatsato, in the Hokoku Maru, was in overall charge of the mission.

The AMCs entered the Malacca Straits as the Bengal and Ondina, blissfully unaware of any potential threat to their safety, were exchanging signals at the rendezvous off Fremantle. As Lt. Cmdr. Wilson had anticipated the Dutch tanker had overstated her speed, and it was at a stately 10 knots that the two set off, the Bengal leading, with the Ondina lumbering along in her wake 400 yards astern. Owing to the swell running, it had been decided not to attempt to transfer the Bengal's missing rating, Able Seaman Henry, and it seemed likely the Australian would have to stay aboard the merchant ship until Diego Garcia was reached.

For the next six days, the two ships steamed north-westwards cocooned in an idyllic world that appeared to be solely theirs. The horizon remained empty, and apart from the ever-present swell – a by-product of the Roaring Forties – the weather was perfect, with blue skies, warm sunshine and zephyr-like winds. Meanwhile, on the other side of the world the war continued unabated. On the beaches of North Africa 90,000 American and British troops were storming ashore, while the German Sixth Army writhed in its own blood before

Stalingrad. In the North Atlantic, the battle with the U-boats moved towards a crescendo, with allied ships going down at the rate of one every 12 hours. For those sailing in the Bengal and Ondina such unpleasantries were hard to comprehend.

At 11.00 on the morning of 11 November, Armistice Day, while flags around the cenotaphs of beleaguered Britain dipped in homage to the dead of two World Wars, the Bengal and Ondina were almost halfway between Fremantle and Diego Garcia and 500 miles SSW of the Cocos Islands. The weather held fine, with the hot sun high in a cloudless sky and the sea a flat calm, its mirror-like surface disturbed only by the lazy bow waves of the two ships steaming in line-ahead at 10 knots and on a course of 299 degrees. The ripples of their feathered wakes stretched back uninterrupted to a horizon as sharp as a whetted knife. This was the Indian Ocean at its best; tranquil and benign.

On the Ondina's bridge, Third Officer Hederik, officer of the watch, paced the starboard wing, his eyes on the horizon. At 11.25, he was about to enter the chartroom to write up the log when a shout from the lookout on the port wing sent him hurrying to that side, snatching the binoculars from their box in the wheelhouse as he passed through.

Following the lookout's pointing finger, Hederik lifted his binoculars and searched the horizon to port. At ten degrees forward of the beam, he found two ships about 8 miles off and on a converging course, steaming at high speed and obviously steering to cross ahead of the Bengal, which was a quarter of a mile ahead of the Ondina. The nearer ship appeared to have an unusually high superstructure similar to that of an aircraft carrier, and Hederik's face grew white under its tan as he dived for the captain's voicepipe.

Captain Horsman came quickly to the bridge and examined the approaching ships through his binoculars. He was aware that no

British or American warships were in the area, and feared the strangers might not be friendly. They had the lines of fast passenger vessels and this could only mean one thing – armed merchant cruisers. The Australian gunlayer Bert Hammond had now reached the bridge and suggested one of the ships might be the Royal New Zealand Navy's AMC Kanimbla. Hammond was familiar with the Kanimbla, a 10,985-ton passenger liner which had regularly plied the Australian coast before the war.

In Horsman's opinion, the short, unraked funnels, clipper bows and cruiser sterns of the ships looked unmistakeably Japanese, but he was prepared to listen to Hammond until the Bengal's signal lamp began to flash urgently. The message was clear: "Enemy in sight. Alter course to 020 degrees." Horsman gave the order to put the helm hard to starboard and reached for the whistle lanyard.

The Ondina's whistle screeched a call to action stations as she and her naval escort swung through 90 degrees to present their sterns to danger. Bengal's yeoman flashed a challenge to the leading ship, which had closed to within 2 miles of the minesweeper. In reply the ship opened fire.

Lieutenant Commander Wilson had no idea of the identity of the attackers or of their armament, but he realised the danger was very great. Without hesitation, he signalled the Ondina to escape to the north-east at all speed, giving her a rendezvous position for 24 hours ahead. Then, with his Indian gun's crew manning the tiny 12-pounder on the minesweeper's bow, Wilson turned the Bengal towards the enemy and rang for full speed.

On the Ondina's bridge, Willem Horsman watched with admiration as the little British warship steamed gallantly towards what must surely be an untimely end. However, he was soon forced to consider the position of his own ship. He found he had only one choice, and that was to make a run for it, futile though the action might be. With all the Hounds of Hell at her heels, the Ondina could not be expected to make more than 12 knots; even then, at the rate the Japanese ships were closing, she was unlikely to get far before being gunned down.

In the wireless room, Radio Officer van Gelderen, acting on Captain Horsman's orders, began to transmit the RRR (Attacked by Raider) signal on the 600 metre band. He repeated this on 17 and 23 metres, hoping to spread the message as wide as possible. But as he pounded his key he could hear his signals being interrupted by transmissions from a nearby source, which could only be the attacking ships. It occurred to van Gelderen as he continued to send, that it mattered little whether his call for help was being heard. Australia lay over a thousand miles to the east, and in this vast ocean Allied warships were as thin on the ground as the tulips in winter.

Right aft, on the Ondina's poop deck, Second Officer Bartele Bakker, in his capacity as gunnery officer, had gathered his mainly British crew around the 4-inch. He could now make out the distinctive OSK funnel markings on the enemy ships and concluded they must have an advantage of 10 knots over the Ondina; their guns would also be heavier and great in number. Bakker had faith in the ability of his gun's crew, but he had no range finder. It would be trial and error from the start, and with only 48 shells in her ammunition locker, the Ondina's chances of survival were, to say the least, poor.

While Bakker deliberated on the fight to come, the little Bengal, her 12-pounder spitting fire, was charging at the leading Japanese ship, the 10,439-ton Hokoku Maru. The range was, as yet, too great for the 12-pounder to have any effect, but Wilson was determined to buy time for the Ondina. It is probable that Commander Imatsato was taken aback by the sheer audacity of the diminutive British warship, for the Hokoku Maru held her fire until the two vessels were less than 3000 yards apart. The Japanese raider's first salvo of 6-inch shells fell 400 yards short of the Bengal's creaming bow-wave, sending a tall column of spray reaching for the sky. On the open bridge of the minesweeper Lieutenant Commander Wilson and his officers tightened the straps of their steel helmets and prepared for the inevitable, Forward, in the bows, the gun captain, Petty Officer Mohd Ibrahim spat on the hot barrel of the 12-pounder and called for maximum elevation.

The Aikoku Maru, hot on the heels of her sister, now entered the fight with her 6-inch guns, and the sea around the Bengal became a maelstrom of bursting shells. Yet, by some miracle, the British ship was not hit and stood on, weaving from side to side like a pugnacious fly-weight facing up to the lumbering advance of two super-heavyweights.

The Ondina, although not yet under fire, was also zig-zagging, her engines producing maximum revolutions. Chief Engineer Jan Niekerk had taken charge in the engine-room and was coaxing the last ounce of power out of the threshing six-cylinder diesel. But the blunt-bowed, broad-beamed tanker was built for commercial reliability rather than speed. Shaking and vibrating from stem to stern, she surged forward until she had worked up to 11 knots, but she could do no more. Looking astern from his bridge and marvelling at the bravery of the Bengal as she faced up to the enemy, Horsman reached the conclusion that running away was no solution.

On the poop deck, in the shadow of the Ondina's belching funnel, Bakker waited for the order to open fire. Muus Visser, perched on the saddle of the 4-inch with his eye glued to the telescope, had the Hokoku Maru firmly sighted, while Bert Hammond, his tanned face impassive, waited with his hand on the trigger. The gun was loaded and primed, and the rest of the crew stood ready to pass shells and gun-cotton charges. Third Engineer Hendrik Leys, acting as messenger, was already on his way forward to report to the bridge.

DEMS Gunners m.v. Odina sitting on gun.
L to R: R. Bayliss (RN); W.R. Lucas (RN); H.C. Boyce (RN); B.B. Bakker 2nd
mate; A/B M. Visser; F. Ryan (RA); on knees: A/B B. Hammond (RAN); W.M.
Nichol (RA); W. Kidd (RA)

The Bengal, now the target of broadsides from both raiders, frequently disappeared from view in the fountains of dirty water thrown up by the shells landing all around her. By the law of averages she must be hit soon, and Horsman debated whether to continue to play the roll of non-combatant or to join in the fight. It was most unlikely the Ondina could escape by running away, but if she showed no aggression the Japanese might allow her crew to abandon ship, unharmed, before they sank her. On the other hand, if she opened up with her 4-inch, there would be no going back; the two raiders would blast her out of the water.

As Horsman weighed up the odds, Hendrik Leys arrived on the bridge to report the after gun closed up, loaded and ready to fire. There was no mistaking the plea in the young engineer's eyes, and when Horsman turned to Maarten Rehwinkel, who was at his side on the bridge, he read the same message. The Ondina must fight.

There had been no relaxation of the state of alert on the poop, and when Leys came racing aft with the order to open fire, Bakker had only to tap the shoulder of the crouching Hammond and the 4-inch thundered out, flame and smoke spurting from its long barrel.

The Ondina's first shell screamed over the Hokoku Maru to land some 400 yards astern of her; with no rangefinder to assist him Bakker was judging the distance by eye. He dropped the range and the second shot fell short, successfully bracketing the raider. For a relatively untried merchant ship's gun's crew this was remarkable shooting. When the 4-inch barked and recoiled for the third time, a red glow was seen high up in the raider's midships superstructure – a direct hit.

The Hokoku Maru now swung round to the north, presenting her starboard side to the Ondina. Commander Imatsato, until then concerned only with the attacking Bengal, had been made forcibly aware of the tanker's intervention and was manoeuvring to give her a broadside with his 6-inch guns. He was too late. Bakker and his crew were loading and laying with the precision of a crack naval gun team. Their fifth shot ploughed into the Hokoku Maru's after deck, causing an enormous explosion. The two catapult-mounted spotter aircraft disappeared in a ball of orange flame and much of the raider's stern disintergrated. To the cheering gunners on the Ondina's poop it seemed they must have hit a "ready use" magazine; in reality, their shell had slammed into a loaded torpedo tube.

Aboard the Bengal, still miraculously unharmed in spite of the shells raining down on her, a cheer was also raised. The minesweeper's crew had not realized the Ondina had joined the fight and were convinced their 12-pounder had caused the damage. But there was no time for self-congratulation, for as the men cheered the Bengal received a direct hit in her forward provision room. The little ship stumbled, then recovered herself, her gun swinging round to engage the Aikoku Maru, which was moving swiftly to the aid of the other raider.

The Hokoku Maru, stopped and on fire aft, turned her guns on the Ondina. Horsman did his utmost to dodge, steering towards the fall of the shot, but within minutes the tanker was hit by a shell, which brought down her main-topmast and wireless aerials. Van Gelderen, who was still bent over his key in the wireless room, saw the current meters of the main aerial drop to zero, switched over to the emergency aerial and continued to transmit a call for help.

As the Ondina came under fire, her Chinese crew panicked and took shelter in the centrecastle under the bridge, where, the tanker's reluctant passenger, Able Seaman Henry, who had no allotted battle station, was on hand to calm the hysterical mob.

The Ondina was hit again and again; one of her starboard lifeboats was smashed and a fire started on her foredeck. The bridge was hit and shrapnel sliced away part of the steering wheel. However, the helmsman Ah Kong stuck to his post, shaming his panic-stricken brothers below the bridge.

The shells crashing around the Ondina created such a curtain of spray that the aim of her gunners became obscured. Hammond called for a cease fire, and while the gun's crew took advantage of the lull with a much-needed cigarette, he and Bakker took stock. As far as they could ascertain, they had scored no fewer than twelve hits on the Hokoku Maru. The whole of her after part was on fire, she was stopped and settling by the stern. Nevertheless, her guns were still firing. Furthermore, the second raider was coming up at speed from the south with the obvious intention of assisting in the Ondina's destruction. The battle promised to be prolonged, and as more than half the tanker's ammunition had been used up, every remaining shell must be made to count. Little help would be forthcoming from the Bengal, for she was seen to be on fire and retiring from the fray.

The situation on board the Bengal was bad, but not as serious as it appeared to those on the poop of the Ondina. The minesweeper had been hit repeatedly and was indeed on fire, but most of the black smoke she was trailing came from her funnel and was being emitted deliberately. With only five rounds of 12-pounder ammunition left in his locker, Lieutenant Commander Wilson had decided to attempt to draw the Aikoku Maru away from the fleeing tanker, which had already put 7 miles between itself and the enemy. There was a chance, albeit a very slim one, that the Ondina might yet escape.

Wilson's gamble came off. The Aikoku Maru gave chase, and for another 15 minutes continued to fire on the Bengal. Then, apparently believing the minesweeper to be crippled and sinking, the raider ceased fire. When, some 20 minutes later, Wilson gave the order to discontinue making smoke, neither raider was in sight and the Ondina was hull-down on the horizon, heading to the south.

The Bengal had been on the receiving end of an estimated 200 shells from the Japanese raiders. She was on fire, severely damaged overall by shrapnel and had a large hole in her starboard bow, above the waterline. Luckily, she had suffered no casualties, and being reasonably sure that the Ondina was making good her escape, Wilson decided the time had come to withdraw from the scene.

Wilson's assumption was wrong, for the Ondina was still very much in the fight. She had resumed firing at the stricken Hokoku Maru but was unable to register any further hits. This was of no consequence, for the fire aboard the raider had spread forward to her main magazine. At 12.30, just over an hour after the two Japanese ships were first sighted, a shattering explosion tore through the Hokoku Maru and she ceased to take any further part in the action.

Another cheer was raised from the Dutch tanker, but this was cut short as the Aikoku Maru, having – as Commander Oishi assumed – dealt with the Bengal, now turned on the Ondina, opening fire from a range of 4000 yards. Her gunlaying was accurate and the fleeing tanker was hit by a salvo of shells that raked her starboard side, inflicting damage to the forecastle head, the bridge and the after pump-room.

At the 4-inch, Bakker and his crew believed the ship was still the target of the Hokoku Maru's guns and wasted four of their precious supply of shells before realising their mistake. When Bakker ordered fire to be switched to the Aikoku Maru, now thundering up on the Ondina's starboard quarter, the tanker's 4-inch was down to 8 rounds.

Hendrik Leys ran through a rain of shrapnel to warn the bridge of the critical situation. Horsman, who had lost sight of the Bengal, and concluded she had been sunk, immediately ordered two smoke floats to be dropped, hoping he might be able to escape under the cover of a smoke screen. Unfortunately, the wind was unfavourable and the Ondina was unable to take shelter behind the smoke and at the same time run away from the raider.

At 12.45, forty minutes after the first shot had been fired in this Armistice Day battle, news was passed to the tanker's bridge that all ammunition for the 4-inch had been expended. It was a sad moment for Willem Horsman. The Ondina had put up a magnificent fight, and, although she had suffered considerable damage, not a man had been killed or injured. She had done her best and to carry on running would be suicidal. The heavily armed Japanese raider would soon overhaul her and pound her until she was a burning wreck. Surrender was now the only option. Horsman instructed Rehwinkel to go below and bring up two large white bedsheets.

When the improvised white flags were flying from the tanker's yardarms, Horsman ordered the lifeboats and rafts to be prepared for launching. Then, with a heavy step he walked to the engine-room telegraph and rang first "Stop," then "Finished With Engines." This was the pre-arranged signal to the engine-room that the ship was being abandoned.

Deep below the waterline, Chief Engineer Jan Niekerk and the resourceful Hendrik Leys, who had joined him, calmly went through the routine of shutting down the main engine and auxiliaries, as they would have done at the end of any passage. Their courage and inbred thoroughness was later to pay a valuable dividend.

Although the Ondina lay stopped in the water with the white flags of surrender clearly displayed at her yardarms, the Aikoku Maru continued to fire on her. Captain Horsman now gave the order to abandon ship, but even as he did so a Japanese shell burst on the starboard side of the bridge and he fell mortally wounded. Command then temporarily passed to Chief Officer Maarten Rehwinkel, who had escaped injury.

In the tanker's wireless room below the bridge, van Gelderen had continued to send out distress signals, using the emergency aerial. But, following this latest hit, his transmitter was put out of action and he knew it was time to leave. Gathering up his log and secret code books, he stuffed them into the specially weighted canvas bag, stepped out onto the boat deck, and hurled the bag overboard. He then climbed to the bridge to report, where he found Rehwinkel attempting to drag Horsman away from the smoking shambles of the starboard wing. Van Gelderen lent a hand, but as the two men gently carried the captain through the wheelhouse, he died of his injuries. The gallant Willem Horsman had relinquished his command for ever.

Rehwinkel and van Gelderen then joined the rest of the tanker's crew at the boats and prepared to abandon ship. Although still under heavy fire from the Aikoku Maru, the three remaining lifeboats and two rafts were launched without mishap. All 56 men left the ship in a matter of three minutes.

Ironically, as the boats and rafts were pulling away from the Ondina, the survivors had the satisfaction of seeing the end of the Hokoku Maru. A final violent explosion ripped through the burning raider, she lifted her bows high in the air and sank out of sight.

The ragged cheer that went up from the boats was cut short, for the Aikoku Maru, her guns still lobbing shells at the deserted Ondina, was bearing down on them at high speed. The tanker men thought that they were about to be taken prisoner, and in view of the reputation of the Japanese, this was not an attractive prospect.

But Commander Oishi had other business in mind. Sweeping up from astern, the Aikoku Maru closed to within about 400 yards of the starboard side of the Ondina and launched two torpedoes. Caught between the enemy and the ship they had abandoned, the tanker's crew watched in horror as the deadly missiles, shark-like in shape and intent, passed a few feet below the keels of their boats and slammed into the Ondina's hull forward of her bridge. Twin columns of water and debris shot high in the air, to be followed by a rumble like thunder. The Ondina shuddered and slowly heeled to starboard, taking up a thirty-degree list.

For the stunned survivors, hunched over their oars, this appeared to be the end of the matter. Their ship was finished and they expected either to be taken prisoner or left to their own devices. Consequently, they were totally unprepared for what happened next.

The Aikoku Maru, having crossed the bows of the Ondina from starboard to port, then swung around the tanker's stern and headed back towards the boats. Rehwinkel and Bakker were first to realise the danger and shouted a warning to the others. They were too late. The Japanese ship opened fire with her heavy machine-guns, raking the lifeboats and the water around them. Those who were quick enough jumped overboard and took cover in the sea; the rest crouched down in the boats with only a thin shell between them and certain death.

Bert Hammond, spreadeagled on the boards of a small life raft, found himself so close to the enemy he was able to take careful note of her armament. She mounted what appeared to be a 6-inch on her forecastle, four similar guns in her forward well deck, four in the after well deck and another on her poop – a total of ten 6-inch guns. On her after deck were two sets of torpedo tubes and two single-engined seaplanes mounted on catapults. Hammond marvelled that the Ondina had lasted so long.

Tamatso Oishi's machine-gunning of the survivors continued for a full ten minutes, until apparently satisfied that he had fully avenged the sinking of the Hokoku Maru, he sheered away and steamed off towards the postion where the other ship had gone down.

No sooner had the raider moved away than the "bodies" floating in the water came back to life and heads appeared above the gunwales of the lifeboats. Mercifully, only two Chinese firemen had been killed by the hail of bullets, but Chief Engineer Niekerk was seriously injured, with a bullet in his head. Able Seaman Richard Henry had a shattered leg and a quartermaster and a fireman were also injured. The three lifeboats were riddled with bullets and all making water. Rehwinkel took charge and ordered all the men to keep out of sight in the bottoms of the boats until the raider had left the scene. The wounded were made as comfortable as possible under the circumstances, but little could be done for Jan Niekerk. At 14.00, he died from his wounds and was committed to the deep with only a scrap of a half-remembered prayer to mark his passing.

Not many minutes had passed after the hurried burial of Niekerk when the Aikoku Maru was seen to be returning and a shiver of fear ran through the boats. It seemed the Japanese were coming back to finish them off – to ensure that no one lived to tell the tale of the rape of the Ondina. But they need not have feared. Commander Oishi, having picked up 278 survivors from the Hokoku Maru's crew of 354, was anxious to leave the area. Ignoring the drifting boats, he passed along the port side of the Ondina and fired a third torpedo at her. Oishi must have been in a desperate hurry, for although the torpedo missed the tanker completely, the Aikoku Maru made off at full speed to the north-east.

It was not until the Japanese ship was out of sight over the horizon that Rehwinkel and Bakker felt safe to make a move. The ragged flotilla of three boats and two rafts had by this time drifted apart and were some 5 miles off the Ondina, which was still afloat, but down by the head and listing heavily. Bakker, who had the motor boat, picked up the men from the rafts, then distributed the 53 survivors more evenly amongst the three boats. The boats then came together and the situation was assessed and discussed.

The prospects for survival were not good. All three lifeboats were badly holed and needed constant bailing – this was serious enough, but not insurmountable. Then it was found that every fresh water tank in the boats had been punctured by bullets and not a drop of drinkable water remained. The nearest land, the Cocos Islands, lay just over 500 miles to the north-east. If the boats were bailed out and repaired, it might be possible to sail to the islands, providing their navigation was good. However, it was most probable that the Cocos were now in Japanese hands, so there seemed little point in attempting the voyage. In any case, without fresh water, they could go nowhere. It was therefore decided that Bakker should take the motor boat back to the Ondina to obtain water and extra provisions before she sank.

Shortly after 16.30, Bartele Bakker brought his boat carefully alongside the Ondina's forward well deck. The tanker's list was frightening, her superstructure pock-marked with shell holes and she was on fire in several places. Bakker was only too aware that reboarding the ship was an extremely hazardous undertaking, there being no guarantee she would not at any moment roll over and make her last plunge to the bottom. He therefore called for volunteers. When he stepped over the Ondina's rail, Bakker had with him Third Engineer Hendrik Leys, the Australian gunlayer Bert Hammond and Bombardier Frank Ryan of the Maritime Regiment, an unflappable Liverpudlian. Third Officer Hederik remained behind to keep an eye on the Chinese ratings, who were just able to keep the boat afloat by continued bailing.

Treading warily on the steeply sloping decks, Bakker and Leys carried out a quick survey of the damage. They ascertained that No.1, 2 and 3 starboard cargo tanks were open to the sea and flooded, also a fire was burning in the fore part of the ship, probably in the paint locker. The fire was not a great threat, and the damage on deck was mainly superficial. On the bridge there was absolute devastation, but when the two officers ventured into the engine-room they had a pleasant surprise. Here there was no flooding and damage was confined to a few shrapnel holes above the waterline; the main engine and its auxiliaries appeared to be untouched. Leys, his eyes gleaming, set the cooling water pumps going, ignored the jets of water spurting from the shrapnel-damaged pipes and started the main engine on air. The big Werkspoor, having been correctly shut down before the ship was abandoned, functioned perfectly.

Damage to Odina's bow

Leys stopped the engine again and the two men, their thoughts running along the same lines, returned to the deck. The list, as far as they could see, had not increased since the Ondina had been torpedoed, indicating the watertight bulkheads forward of the bridge were holding. If the ship could be returned to the upright, there was a definite possibility of getting her under way again. There remained, however, the question of stability; if water was run into the port side tanks to correct the list, this might tip the balance and cause the ship to capsize. After a brief consultation with the two gunners, Bakker and Leys decided the risk was worth taking. Battered though she might be, the Ondina was the best lifeboat on offer to them.

Working with great care, and always ready to make a quick dash for the ship's rail should the worst happen, the four men opened the port side deck valves allowing the sea to flood into the empty tanks. Slowly, very slowly, the list started to come off and within an hour the tanker was once more near to the upright, but not without a price being paid. The hundreds of tons of water run into the port tanks had the inevitable result of putting the ship so low in the water that the sea was within a foot of her main deck.

Having established the tanker was not about to sink, Bakker despatched the motor boat to bring the other boats alongside. Accompanied by Leys, he then went to the bridge and the two men carried the body of Captain Horsman to his cabin. The Ondina awaited her new master.

By 19.00, all the survivors were back on board the Ondina and Maarten Rehwinkel had assumed command. The lifeboats were carefully hoisted on board and stowed on deck; there was no knowing when they might be needed again. The small fires on deck were easily extinguished, but the blaze raging in the fore part had spread to the Ondina's precious cargo of grain and this fire was only subdued by a superhuman effort on the part of the British gunners. Meanwhile, Second Engineer Adriaan Brevet had taken charge of the engine-room and by 21.00 the engine was ready to start and the emergency steering gear had been rigged. At this point fire flared up again in the cargo of grain and it was after midnight before it was under control. The Ondina finally got under way, heading for Fremantle, at 00.40 on the 12th.

The sun had begun its long climb from the eastern horizon before the shambles on the tanker's bridge was cleared, enabling the telemotor steering gear to be repaired and brought back into use. Under the careful hands of Acting Chief Engineer Brevet, the main engine functioned well, although for the time being Brevet was not prepared to increase to full revolutions. However, the battle-scarred tanker, steering a south-easterly course, was on her way back to her adopted home, knowing the 1,400-mile passage to Fremantle would not be easy. With some of her tanks open to the sea and her freeboard little more than a couple of hand's-breadths, any bad weather could prove disastrous. Navigation would be of the most primitive, for the ship's only chronometer had been smashed during the shelling. Latitude could be checked each day at noon, but Rehwinkel would have no means of determining the longitude. He would have to rely on a method used by his predecessors centuries ago, running south-eastwards until he reached the latitude of Fremantle, and then due east until the port came in sight. And, of course, there was always the possibility that the Aikoku Maru might come looking for them again. If this happened, the Ondina would not be given a second chance.

At 20.00 that night, the Ondina was stopped and Captain Willem Horsman, his body shrouded in canvas, was committed to the deep by the men he had died to save. When he was gone and the passage resumed, it was time to attend to the injured. Richard Henry, whose leg had been shattered, was in a serious condition, and the two injured Chinese ratings also urgently required medical attention. On the 13th, van Gelderen, having repaired his aerials, transmitted a message to all stations asking for medical assistance. In the absence of code books, which had been dumped over the side before abandoning ship, the message was sent in plain language, but omitting the ship's position. The transmission was acknowledged by Perth, but no reply was forthcoming from the Australian station. Colombo was contacted on the 15th, again without revealing the ship's position, and with a similar result. It seemed the authorities ashore were highly suspicious of this ship claiming to be the Ondina but which was ignorant of the secret codes. It might well be a trap to lure rescue ships into the waiting arms of the Japanese. Perth asked the Ondina to give her position in plain language, but Rehwinkel, also wary of being trapped, refused to do so. And so a ridiculous stalemate was reached, and all the time Richard Henry became weaker through loss of blood. It began to look as though the machine-gunners of the Aikoku Maru were about to claim another victim.

The tragic farce came to an end when, on the morning of the 17th, the Ondina, then only 220 miles north-west of Fremantle, was sighted by a patrolling Catalina. Messages were exchanged by Aldis lamp and a few hours later Richard Henry was taken on board a nearby Australian hospital ship, where his life was saved by blood transfusions. At 10.00 on the morning of 18 November, with her ensign flying at half-mast for her dead, the battered Ondina entered Fremantle harbour. Twenty-four hours earlier, the gallant Bengal had also reached a safe haven in Diego Garcia.

Long after the dust of this unique sea battle had settled, the inevitable inquiries, official and unofficial, began. From the Dutch side, the actions of the Bengal were questioned. She was accused of running away, leaving the Ondina to her fate, but there is little evidence to back this accusation. The minsweeper had achieved what Lieutenant Commander Wilson set out to do, and that was to draw the enemy's fire for as long as possible, so that the tanker might escape. When the Bengal ceased to make smoke, the Japanese ships were no longer in sight and the Ondina was apparently escaping to the south. It is quite understandable that Wilson assumed she had got away. In any case, with her ammunition almost exhausted, the Bengal was in no fit state to re-enter the fight. Criticism – this from the Admiralty – was also levelled at Captain Horsman for joining battle with the raiders when he had been ordered by Wilson to run away. But Willem Horsman was no coward and, like all master mariners, resented the threat to his ship. Unfortunately, his Nelsonian gesture cost him his life, but it did result in the sinking of the Hokoku Maru and, in turn, undoubtedly saved the little Bengal from being pounded to pieces.

As to the outcome of the Indian Ocean battle of 11 November 1942 there can be no doubt. It was a major defeat for the Japanese armed merchant cruisers, and the culmination of a far from distinguished career. The Hokoku Maru and Aikoku Maru, the first of their kind, had accounted for only five ships of a total of 31,342 tons, and this for the loss of the 10,439-ton Hokoku Maru and 76 of her crew, including Commander Hirishi Imatsato. It was an experiment never to be repeated by the Japanese Imperial Navy.

FOUR

In April 1942, American B-25s led by Lieutenant Colonel James H. Doolittle, bombed Tokyo for the first time. The damage inflicted was negligible but the effect on Japanese morale enormous. Two months later, near a tiny Pacific island called Midway, close to the International Date Line, the Japanese Imperial Navy received a hammering from which it was never to fully recover. Two thirds of Admiral Nagumo's crack carrier force, responsible for much of the humiliation of the Allied fleets in the early days of the war, was wiped out in a single action. As the year came to a close, it was obvious the surging tide of Japanese conquest, which had engulfed much of the old colonial empires of Britain, France and Holland and lapped at the northern shores of Australia, had reached its peak.

The debacle of Midway was soon followed by the landing of American troops on Guaducanal, easternmost outpost of the new empire of Nippon. By February 1943, after a long and bloody conflict, the last Japanese soldier was expelled from this island fortress and Allied forces embarked on a relentless march back to the west. But, for the Japanese people the bitterest blow of all fell when the cherry blossoms of Kyushu were in full bloom. On 18 April, Admiral Yamamoto's plane was intercepted over the jungles of Bougainville by American P-38s and sent crashing to the ground in flames. Next to Emperor Hirohito, Isoroku Yamamoto was perhaps the greatest contemporary legend of Japanese invincibility, and his loss at the hands of a despised enemy caused shockwaves of grief to resound throughout Japan. On 22 April, General MacArthur, striking north from Port Moresby, began the final battle to liberate New Guinea, a battle that was to result in very heavy casualties on both sides.

On 12 May 1943, His Majesty's Australian Hospital Ship Centaur sailed from Sydney, bound for Port Moresby to evacuate sick and injured. She had on board 283 Australian Army Medical Corps personnel, including 12 nurses, and a Torres Strait pilot to guide her through the intricacies of the Great Barrier Reef. Her hospital beds were made up, her theatres prepared to deal with the unavoidable results of war, but there was not a man or woman aboard who believed their involvement would go beyond that.

Built in Greenock in 1924 for the Australia-Singapore service of the Blue Funnel Line of Liverpool, the 3222-ton Centaur had spent 16 years on this run, providing a popular and valuable cargo/passenger link between the Antipodes and the Malayan peninsular. In March 1943 she was commandeered by the Admiralty and converted to a hospital ship. She then came under the wing of the Royal Australian Navy, but retained her merchant service crew of 76 British officers and ratings. In command was 54-year-old Captain George Murray, a Scot settled in Australia. The Centaur's 2000 horse power Burmeister & Wain diesel engine, which gave her a top speed of 14 knots, was in the charge of Chief Engineer A. Jackson, also 54, and a Tynesider.

At 04.00 on the morning of 14 May, the Centaur was 40 miles east of Brisbane and heading north for the Torres Strait. The weather was fine, with only a light northerly breeze rippling the tops of a moderate swell rolling in from the north-east. Overhead, bright stars showed intermittently through gaps in a broken canopy of cloud that promised to disappear with the coming of the sun. It was the darkest hour before the dawn when the world lies hushed and sombre, gathering its strength to meet the unknown challenges of a new day.

Although wrapped around with the darkness of the night, the Centaur was a blaze of light, a rare sight in the Pacific in those embattled days. She was illuminated as required of a hospital ship in accordance with Article 5 of the Hague Convention, carrying, in addition to her navigation lights, large floodlit red crosses on each side of her hull and funnel, on the fore side of her bridge and on her stern facing aft. Streamers of brilliant white lights along the sides of her white-painted hull drew attention to a wide band of green running from stem to stern, also as required by the Convention. There could be no mistaking that the Centaur was an unarmed ship on a mission of mercy. But should there still be any doubt of this, notification of her presence in these waters and her description in full had been communicated to the Japanese Government by the Australian authorities in February of that year.

As eight bells rang out, the watches were changing on the bridge of the Centaur, Second Officer R.G. Rippon handing over to his relief, Chief Officer Henry Lamble. The two men conversed in low tones for a short while, then Rippon said a belated goodnight and went below to resume his interrupted sleep. Left alone on the bridge, Henry Lamble, a 31-year-old Devonian, waited for the dawn to come.

The ship was steering due north at 12 knots and the loom of the light on Point Lookout, 24 miles to the west, was just visible on the horizon. All was quiet. Below the bridge, on the promenade deck, the doctors and nurses were comfortably asleep in the passenger cabins, while the other ranks of the medical unit occupied harder bunks in the forward 'tween decks, all gathering their strength for the grim task to come. Only the rumble of the engine and the creak of the wheel as it responded to the hand of the helmsman reminded Lamble that he was not completely alone. He gazed out to sea, straining his eyes to pierce the darkness. Although the floodlights in the bows had been switched off to improve visibility from the bridge, the bright glow emanating from the array of other lights made it impossible to see the line of the horizon. Lamble – and most of his fellow crew members would have agreed with him – was not at all happy with this state of affairs. It was all very well for the Centaur to comply with the Convention and illuminate herself like a giant Christmas Tree, but what guarantee was there the enemy would also abide by the rules? There were times during the dark watches when Henry Lamble felt he was sitting astride the proverbial sacrificial lamb being led through a den of hungry lions.

Lieutenant-Commander H. Nakagawa, in the conning tower of I-177, had a very different view of the night. Cruising on the surface just outside the circle of light cast by the Centaur, the Japanese submarine was trimmed down with her casings awash, betraying her presence only by the darker shadow she cast and the blue-green phosphoresence of her bow wave. To the lookouts on the ship she stalked she was completely invisible.

Built at Sasebo in late 1942, I-177 was one of the Imperial Navy's smaller ocean-going submarines, displacing only 1500 tons. She carried a crew of 86, had a maximum surface speed of 23 knots and was capable of cruising for 8000 miles without refuelling. Her armament consisted of one 12-cm deck gun, one 25-mm, twin-barrelled anti-aircraft cannon and 12 torpedoes. She left Tokyo Bay with Nakagawa in command in early February 1943, and arrived off Guaducanal in time to witness the last stand of the Japanese garrison on the island. She then moved to the east coast of Australia to begin operations in company with three other boats of her class. For Nakagawa, an officer passionately dedicated to the furtherance of Japan's military aims in the Pacific, the patrol so far had been a dismal failure, enlivened only by the sinking of the British motor vessel Limerick 100 miles south of Brisbane on 25 April. The next nineteen days spent combing the coastal waters of Queensland had proved fruitless, and when in the pre-dawn hours of 14 May, the plainly illuminated and marked Allied hospital ship came into view, Nakagawa had already thrown away the book of rules. As the 4 to 8 watch settled down on the Centaur, I-177 sank to periscope depth and prepared her tubes for firing.

The torpedo struck the unsuspecting Centaur on her port side forward of the bridge. It penetrated well below the waterline near the bottom of her No.3 deep tank, used to carry cargoes of vegetable oils in less hostile days, but now part-full with fuel oil. The force of the explosion was devastating, throwing burning oil over the fore part of the bridge and superstructure. Within seconds, the whole of the Centaur's accommodation and bridge was a mass of flames.

Second Officer Rippon had undressed and was preparing to turn in when the torpedo hit at precisely 04.15. He threw on a few clothes, and with the stench of burning oil in his nostrils and the screams of the dying assaulting his ears, he reached the deck clutching his life-jacket and intent on reporting to the bridge. As he was about to climb the bridge ladder, Henry Lamble came stumbling down. The chief officer had been blinded by the flames. Captain Murray also appeared on deck, but Rippon lost sight of him in the choking clouds of black smoke rolling over the ship from forward to aft. Shortly afterwards, the bridge collapsed and the funnel crashed down on top of it.

Adopting the only logical course in the circumstances, Rippon retreated to the boat deck, where he found himself alone. He was in the act of attempting to lower one of the lifeboats single-handed when the Centaur lurched heavily to port and sank bow first, the surrounding sea turning to hissing steam as it quenched the burning oil.

Approximately three minutes had elapsed since Nakagawa's torpedo struck home.

When Rippon came gasping to the surface, he found himself treading water in a sea strewn with wreckage but mercifully free of flames. All around him he saw tiny red lifejacket lights and heard plaintive cries for help. Now he was no longer alone.

Although it appeared a great number had survived the sinking of the Centaur, the hospital ship had gone down so quickly there was little left for them to cling to. Rippon's first thought was of the voracious hammer-headed sharks that roamed these warm waters in great numbers. Near to panic, he kicked out, seeking a raft, a hatchboard – anything on which to lift his vulnerable body out of the sea.

At last, the sky paled in the east, and as is the pattern in the tropics, the sun mounted the horizon without delay. Rippon found sanctuary on a crowded raft, one of two that had come to the surface when the ship sank. Two lifeboats had also floated clear, but one of these was capsized and the other swamped. From his precarious platform Rippon was able to estimate about 200 survivors around him, some clinging to the other raft and the boats, but the majority drifting aimlessly amongst the wreckage over a wide area of the sea.

The realisation of the hopelessness of their position began to dawn on Rippon. The Centaur had gone down so quickly it was extremely unlikely the radio officer on watch – assuming he had survived the blast – had been able to send out an SOS. There was some possibility a watcher on shore may have seen the brief conflagration preceeding the hospital ship's sudden end, but then few will have been abroad on the Queensland coast at such an early hour in the morning. No – the reality was, that if the sinking had been seen or heard, the rescue ships would have been on the scene by daylight. Rippon felt a great wave of depression sweeping over him.

At 11.30, with the sun nearing its zenith and blazing down fiercely on the pathetic remnants of the Centaur's complement, a four-engined flying boat – Rippon identified it as a Catalina – flew overhead at about 5000 feet but gave no sign of having seen them. Fifteen minutes later, a tanker was sighted passing 5 miles to seaward, and the men on the raft raised a cheer. They might as well have saved their parched throats, for the ship also ignored them.

The rest of the day passed without further sightings and the spirits of the survivors slid into decline. Torrential showers before dusk did something to alleviate their thirst, and the return of darkness brought a respite from the hot sun, but it also lessened their chances of being seen. Then, in the early hours of the 15th, the throb of diesel engines was heard echoing across the silent waters. The sound came nearer and was identifiable to Rippon as a submarine passing some 2 miles off the raft. Crew Cook Martin, floating on three hatch gratings, was later able to confirm this. The submarine passed within a quarter of a mile of Martin, and he estimated her to be about 300 feet in length, with one gun forward of the conning tower and a flat structure aft, possibly an aircraft hanger. I-177 had returned to the scene of her crime.

A number of aircraft flew over during that day, but they were merely passing by en route. No one, it appeared, was searching for survivors from the Centaur. Then, at 14.00, when Rippon and his companions on the raft were resigning themselves to yet another night of misery, a patrolling aircraft and a destroyer were sighted. The few smoke floats the raft carried were set off and produced immediate results. But when the destroyer, USS Mugford, reached the area, she picked up only 64 survivors, made up of 29 of the Centaur's crew, her Torres Strait pilot, and 34 medical personnel, including one nurse. Of the hospital ship's total complement of 360, no less than 296, including 11 nurses, had gone down with the ship, died of exposure, or been taken by sharks.

When the full horror of the sinking of the Centaur became known, the following note was sent to the Japanese Government through diplomatic channels:

"His Majesty's Government in the Commonwealth of Australia most emphatically protests to the Japanese Government against this wanton attack in disregard not only of the Hague Convention and of International Law, but also of the principles of common humanity accepted by all civilised nations. The Commonwealth Government demands that those responsible for the attack should be punished immediately and demands assurance from the Japanese Government that there will be no repetition by the Forces under the command of the Japanese Government of such an incident in violation of International Law and practice. The Commonwealth Government reserves the right to claim full indemnification and redress for losses sustained."

As was to be expected, this protest fell on deaf ears. The Imperial Japanese Navy had its own ideas on how the war at sea should be fought, and Lieutenant-Commander Nakagawa, once blooded, was to be its arch exponent in the art of slaughtering defenceless merchant seamen.

I-177, under the command of Lieutenant Katsuji Watanabe, was sunk with all hands by the destroyer USS Samuel S. Miles off the Palau Islands on 3 October 1944. By then Nakagawa had already moved to I-37, in which he continued his bloody career.

FIVE

When, on 16 January 1942, Japan invaded Burma, British forces in that brooding land of mountain and forest were, in not unfamiliar pattern, quickly overrun. The Japanese commanded overwhelming superiority in the air, and with the Royal Navy retired in disarray to East Africa, held absolute sway over the India Ocean. By mid-May, British and Indian troops, fighting a desperate rearguard action, had been rolled back across the Chindwin to the frontiers of India. For a long while it seemed the great empire of the Raj itself was threatened, but, fortunately, the Japanese found themselves with their supply lines dangerously extended and were forced to call a halt. There followed a year-long stalemate, during which the British 14th Army doggedly held fast at the frontier with India, the Japanese consolidated their gains in Burma, and American aircraft flying over the "Hump" of the Himalayas kept supplied a largely ineffectual Chinese 5th Army in the north. For the Allies it was at best only a holding operation, but such were the demands on their resources in other theatres, it was all they could then manage.

In August 1943, when Lord Louis Mountbatten took over the newly formed South East Asia Command (SEAC), sufficient forces had been built up to lay plans for Operation "Anakim," the return to Burma of the Allies. This invasion, by land and sea, was scheduled to take place in late December 1943 or early January 1944, when the dry north-east monsoon would be fully established. Much of the success of the operation would depend on sea-borne supplies channelled in through the Indian port of Chittagong, on the north-east coast of the Bay of Bengal, and only 60 miles from the border with Burma.

The main body of Admiral Somerville's Eastern Fleet returned from the shelter of Mombasa Island to Colombo in September, but was still only a rather pitiful collection of old cruisers and armed merchantmen, led by the battleship Ramillies, a veteran of the First World War. Somerville had no aircraft carriers, and apart from the slow and lightly armed AMCs, precious few ships available for convoy escort work. Fortunately, by November there were only, at the most, one or two German U-boats operational in the Indian Ocean. Of the Japanese submarines, whose capability appeared to be limited, it was believed there were still eight at large, but these were scattered over a very wide area. Allied merchant ships were, therefore, sailing in convoy only in areas of high risk, these being mainly the approaches to the Gulf of Aden and the Persian Gulf.

It was thus that, on 27 November 1943, the 4087-ton British cargo steamer Daisy Moller left Bombay, bound for Chittagong, her only escort being the flying fish that frollicked in her bow wave. But the great brooding hump of Bombay's Elephanta Island was hardly out of sight before even they deserted her, for these tiny winged creatures quickly lose interest in a slow-moving object. And slow-moving the Daisy Moller was, without any doubt. Built in 1911, at a time when the last of the windjammers were still flogging their way around the Horn, she left Bremer Vulkan's yard on the Weser bearing the name

Pindos and went into service with the Deutsche Levant Line. During the First World War, she was taken as a prize by the Royal Navy, and in 1917 handed over to the Gem Line of Glasgow and renamed Huntscape. After the war, she appeared in the Far East under the name Wilfred, and in 1934 was bought by Moller & Company Limited, a British-owned shipping company trading exclusively in the Far East and based in Shanghai. By the time war came along again in 1939, the quaintly named Daisy Moller had had a long and profitable life in the hands of her various owners and should have been on the verge of banishment to the breaker's yard. But the demands of war are ever great on shipping and she was obliged to plod on. In November 1943, she was 32 years old, carrying more than her fair share of rust, and on a good day capable of a maximum speed of 8œ knots.

Despite her obvious faults, the Daisy Moller was as seaworthy and well-run as any ship under the Red Ensign. Commanded by 40-year-old Captain Reginald Weeks of Kingskerwell in Devon, she carried a total crew of 71, including Indian ratings on deck and Chinese in the engine-room. Her officers, as was often the custom in a British ship based in the Far East, were a cosmopolitan lot, men who through choice or force of circumstances, had put down temporary roots in the East. Chief Officer Harold Hoyer hailed from Norway, Second Officer Kuzma Nicolaeff was an exile from the Czar's Russia, Third Officer Peter Jorgensen came from Denmark and Second Engineer Gulko Joseph from Poland. Chief Engineer J.F. Palmer and Radio Officer Patrick Healy were British, while the only "local" was Third Engineer Fu Yuen Sung. Most were men who had a preference for the Orient, where the pace was slower, living cheap and the climate kind – and who could blame them?

The Daisy Moller's "odd men out," serving at His Majesty's behest, were her six DEMS gunners, Able Seaman Gunlayer Charles Dillon, Able Seaman Richard Casson, Able Seaman James Porter all of the

Royal Navy, and Lance Bombardier Eric Clark and Gunners Sibson and Wombwell of the Royal Artillery's Maritime Regiment. These men, while enjoying the comparatively relaxed discipline of a merchant ship, maintained and manned the Daisy Moller's accoutrements of war; an ancient 4-inch, two 20 mm Oerlikons and four light machine-guns. They were confident about using this modest armament to good effect if called upon to do so, but being for the most part down-to-earth North Country men, they had no illusions about what would happen, should they meet up with the enemy. Heavily loaded and proceeding at the pace of an elderly carthorse, the Daisy Moller presented a target to set any professional gunner drooling with delight. The fight, if and when it came, would be short and painfully one sided.

DEMS Gunners aboard Daisy Moller Calcutta 1942.
Two men in Pith helmets are from Louise Moller

With the low-lying Malabar Coast in sight to port, the Daisy Moller steamed south through a placid sea dotted with fleets of idling fishing canoes. The weather was typical for the time of the year; hot and humid, with cloudless skies periodically darkened by huge cumulonimbuses swollen with rain, left over from the retreating South-West Monsoon. The war seemed light years away, yet Captain Reginald Weeks was uneasy as he walked the bridge of his ageing command with a faint breeze ruffling his hair. Navigationally, the 2,300-mile passage to Chittagong, including a brief call at Colombo, held no fears for him. He had travelled this way many times before and knew by name every headland, every distant peak; was familiar with every quirk of the treacherous currents that washed these deceptively beautiful shores. But the Daisy Moller's holds were crammed with enough military stores, including ammunition, to supply several regiments of fighting troops, the loading of which had been witnessed by far too many curious eyes. Anti-British feeling was running high in India, and word of the ship's sailing must have already reached the Japanese. That the Admiralty had assured him the area was virtually clear of the enemy, cut no ice with Weeks.

After a longer than expected stay in Colombo, the Daisy Moller on 8 December, having taken on two passengers, Lieutenant Fisher of the North West African Frontier Force and his African bearer, who were on their way to the Burma front, via Chittagong. The direct route to Chittagong, after rounding the southern tip of Ceylon, lay north-easterly across the Bay of Bengal, a deep-water passage of some 1,250 miles. However, perhaps in receipt of disturbing intelligence, or merely apprehensive at sending such a vulnerable ship, unescorted across this open stretch of water, the Admiralty in Colombo had instructed Weeks to take a more devious route. He was advised to hug the Indian coast all the way to the head of the bay, before striking across for Chittagong. This would add at least 200 miles to the passage, but presumably Their Lordships hoped the relatively shallow water, close inshore, would be free of enemy submarines. Although he would have

prefered the more direct route, Weeks was anxious not to tempt fate –
much less the Japanese Imperial Navy. The recommended "rock dodg-
ing" might be an added strain on the nerves of those who kept the
bridge watches, but the Daisy Moller would set her courses to closely
follow the curve of the coast.

Daisy Moller coaling ship, Calcutta 1942

The first setback of the passage came after rounding Dondra Head,
the southernmost point of Ceylon, when an inshore current setting
south in excess of 2 knots was encountered – a severe hindrance to an
8œ-knot ship. This current persisted as they moved north, and there
were times when Weeks was sorely tempted to head out into deeper
waters to avoid it, but, in view of the warnings he had received in
Colombo, the adverse current seemed to be the lesser of two evils. In
the early hours of 14th, six days out from Ceylon, having averaged a
shade under 6 knots, the Daisy Moller was off Sacramento Shoal, a
hard finger of sand jutting out to sea from the coast 240 miles north

of Madras. Some 650 miles still remained to go to Chittagong, but the current was beginning to slacken noticeably.

When Captain Weeks appeared on the bridge just after four o'clock that morning, Chief Officer Harold Hoyer, who had just taken over the watch, was able to report the ship was back up to her normal 8œ knots. It was two hours before daylight, the morning fine and clear, with only a gentle north-easterly breeze rippling the sea. In the west, a giant yellow moon hung low in a star-filled sky, its brilliant light picking out the dark shoulders of the Eastern Ghats, which slope down to the densely wooded coastal plain fronting the Bay of Bengal. The scent of the land, only 3 miles distant, was heavy in the air; a heady mixture of rotting vegetation and pungent spices overlaid with the occasional waft of wood smoke, for the cooking fires of India are alight early. To Weeks, these brief hours before the rays of the tropical sun turned the ship into a superheated sweatbox were the best of the day.

The early morning scene was so tranquil, and the threat of war so remote, that both Weeks and Hoyer were in a confident mood as they chatted quietly in the port wing of the bridge. Having steamed over 1,600 miles with no sign of the enemy, and with journey's end a mere three days away, the omens for the completion of an uneventful passage were good, with the prospect of spending Christmas and New Year in port. Not that Chittagong, hot, dirty, with mosquitoes the size of dragon flies, had much to offer. But at least, safely berthed 10 miles up the Karnaphuli River, they would have the opportunity to relax – a rare privilege in these danger-filled days.

In the wireless room abaft the bridge, Radio Officer Patrick Healy yawned and eased the headphones back from his ears. On watch from 04.00, he had listened in on all the relevant frequencies but the ether was as quiet as the grave – not an unusual state of affairs, considering the time of the day, the place and the constrictions of war on radio communications. The next two hours promised to be equally boring, relieved only by the crackle of atmospherics and the arrival of the steward with tea and toast at 05.30.

For Lieutenant Kazuro Ebato, on the other hand, the adrenalin was running. Crouched at the periscope of RO-110, submerged close on the unsuspecting Daisy Moller's starboard bow, he waited impatiently for the long hours of careful stalking to reach their climax. RO-110, a small submarine of only 525 tons displacement, was a long way from the coastal waters of Japan, which she had been built to defend. Carrying just eight torpedoes and having a surface speed of only 16 knots, she could hardly be described as a front-line unit of the Japanese Imperial Navy, but for the job in hand, an attack in shallow water, she was well fitted.

Slowly, the dark silhouette of the Daisy Moller crept into the light of the setting moon and Ebato rapped out the order to fire. The 21-inch torpedo, carrying a 900 lb warhead, sped through the water at 49 knots, silent, swift and deadly.

The first pale fingers of approaching dawn were lightening the eastern sky when, at 04.20, the torpedo slammed into the Daisy Moller's starboard side, exploding with a dull roar. A sheet of flame erupted from between her two forward hatchways, followed by a gusher of dirty water and debris reaching to mast-top height. She immediately took a heavy list to starboard.

In the Daisy Moller's wireless room the force of the explosion blew Patrick Healy from his chair and he crashed painfully against the deck-head of the cabin, before falling to the deck in a heap. Partly stunned, his reactions thereafter, rehearsed so many times in his mind on the long, empty watches, were purely automatic. Retrieving his headphones, he switched on the main transmitter, tuned it to the distress frequency and tapped out the emergency signal SSS (I am being attacked by a submarine), the ship's position and her secret call sign, repeating the sequence four times. Fortunately, his message was picked up by an alert operator at the radio station at Vizagapatam, 130 miles to the north.

On the bridge, Weeks and Hoyer recovered quickly from the initial shock of the torpedoing. Within seconds, the ship was down by the head and listing dangerously. There was no immediate sign of fire in the holds, but mindful of the ammunition they were carrying, Weeks instructed Hoyer to prepare to abandon ship. The Daisy Moller was well provided with lifeboats and life rafts, and with the land only 3 miles to port, the prospects for survival were good.

Unfortunately, the ship had been hit when most of her crew were still deep in sleep – it was that dreary hour before dawn, when human life is said to be at its lowest ebb. Tumbling out onto the deck, dazed and half-clothed, men made their way to the boat deck, their movements confused and panic not far below the surface. In the dark and the urgency of the moment, the rope falls of one of the lifeboats were prematurely released and the boat plummeted to the water and was smashed. Luckily, no men were on board when it fell.

The dying ship had by then assumed a massive 50 degree list to starboard, so the struggle to lower the three remaining lifeboats was both exhausting and and fraught with danger, for no one knew when the Daisy Moller might suddenly capsize. But, under the steadying influence of Weeks and his deck officers, the boats were launched and boarded. Gunlayer Charles Dillon and his men, whose accommodation was aft, made no attempt to reach the boat deck, preferring to launch the wooden life rafts stowed in the after rigging.

The hurried evacuation was not a moment too soon. Three minutes after the last boat pulled clear of her side the Daisy Moller lifted her stern high and slipped below the waves, bow first. Standing in the stern sheets of his boat, Reginald Weeks watched the passing of his command with a lump in his throat. She had been old and cranky, but always compliant. He would miss her.

A rough head-count was made and it was established that, miraculously, no one had gone down with the ship. The only casualty appeared to be Able Seaman Richard Casson, who had sustained a badly scalded leg and a sprained ankle. It could have been much worse. Then, without warning, the unnatural silence of the night was disturbed by a loud hissing and RO-110 surfaced only 100 yards away. As he watched the long, ghostly shape rising from the depths, Weeks was already ripping off his epaulettes of rank. It was common knowledge that Axis submarines were in the habit of taking the masters of torpedoed merchant ships out of circulation, and he had no wish to rot in a prisoner of war camp.

The submarine's diesels thundered into life and she turned short round and headed for the boats. Shadowy figures were clearly visible on her casings and in the conning tower. Weeks steeled himself for the interrogation to come and hoped his anonymity would be preserved. Then, the submarine's bow wave began to foam as she quickly worked up speed and the awful truth became apparent. She intended to ram.

It was too late for Weeks to take action. The sharp prow of the 500-ton submarine caught the wooden lifeboat squarely amidships, slicing through its brittle timbers like the blade of a sharpened axe and spilling men into the sea in all directions. Ebato then backed his command away from the splintered wreckage and deliberately opened fire with a machine-gun on the men in the water. As the tracers scythed towards them, Weeks and his crew frantically sought cover below the surface, but few succeeded.

Ebato then turned on the other boats, callously ramming them in similar fashion and using his machine-gun with the same terrifying effect. Having dealt with them, the Japanese commander directed his fire at the life rafts, two of which were supporting the Daisy Moller's gunners. These rafts were of a double-sided construction, with a well top and bottom designed to give space for the occupants legs and feet, whichever way up they hit the water. The injured Richard Casson and Lance Bombardier Eric Clark saved their lives by diving over the side and taking refuge in the lower well of their raft, which acted as an air pocket for their heads. The others were not so fortunate. When the sun finally climbed over the horizon, the screams had stopped and the waters surrounding the grave of the Daisy Moller were red with the blood of her crew.

In Vizagapatam, 130 miles to the north, where Patrick Healy's SOS had been picked up, a frantic search was under way to find a suitable vessel to go to the aid of the Daisy Moller. In any other part of the world it is probable an Allied warship would have at once left harbour with a bone in her teeth and all her guns manned. However, this was India and the year 1943. All that could be found for the rescue mission was the tug Zerang, a slow, ancient and unarmed craft. She was hastily chartered by the Admiralty, and with the Vizagapatam naval pilot, Lieutenant Lewis Maxwell-Clarkson, RINVR, on board, steamed south at her best possible speed.

Late that night, when the Zerang arrived off Sacramento Shoal, a large cluster of tiny red lights was seen floating on the water. Maxwell-Clarkson at once recognised these as lifejacket lights, and assumed they had found survivors. Disllusionment came swiftly, and with it horror and revulsion. As the tug steamed slowly through the bobbing lights no evidence of life was visible and bodies pulled from the water for examination were found to be riddled by bullets. Out of a total of 71 men, who had abandoned the Daisy Moller with such high hopes of survival, 55 lay dead with their faces to the sea.

Maxwell-Clarkson was puzzled that no sign could be found of the ship's officers, neither were any lifeboats or rafts to be seen. This indicated to him that some men may have reached the shore, and at first light on the 15th he took the Zerang into the coast and landed with a search party. It was three days before he found Captain Weeks and fifteen others being looked after by the District Magistrate at Masulipatam. Their story was not a pleasant one.

Thrown from the lifeboat by the force of the collision, Weeks escaped the bullets that followed by hiding behind the wreckage of the boat. When the submarine left the scene, he swam to a raft and was there joined by eleven others. With the coming of full daylight two more rafts were seen close by, and another survivor joined their ranks. Weeks again took up the burden of command and distributed his men amongst the three rafts, all of which were damaged. He then took stock of the situation. With him were Chief Engineer J.F. Palmer, Second Officer Kuzma Nicolaeff, Radio Officer Patrick Healy, Third Engineer Fu Yuen Sung, the gunners Richard Casson and Eric Clark, and seven Indian ratings. They were a sorry sight, some wounded, all partially clothed, suffering from exposure, and in a state of shock. And they were the lucky ones. As far as Weeks could ascertain, the remaining members of his crew were beyond help.

But this was no time to mourn the dead. The land was in sight to the west and Weeks was determined that, having survived thus far, these men would not perish at sea. The rafts were cumbersome and partly waterlogged, but using oars and canvas awnings rigged as sails, they set off, confident they would reach land before dark.

As luck would have it, the ragged fleet came under the influence of the same southerly drift that had delayed the Daisy Moller's progress and it was midnight on the 17th before they finally came ashore on the sand dunes of the Krishna River delta. Swept into a bight in the coast by the current, they had covered almost 80 miles in a west-south-westerly direction. On that same day, fishermen casting their nets six miles offshore came upon across the broken remains of a lifeboat. Draped across it were three of the Daisy Moller's Indian crew, suffering severely from exposure, but still alive. On the 18th they joined the others at Masulipatam.

Two months later, RO-110 was still combing the sea off Vizagapatam, but had not yet increased her meagre score. Kazuro Ebato's oriental patience was wearing thin when he sighted a small convoy and crept in to attack. His first torpedo damaged the British steamer Asphalion but also brought the convoy escort in, with depth charges flying. Before the hour was up the crumpled remains of RO-110 lay on the bottom, a fitting tomb for Ebato and his men. The killing of the Daisy Moller had been avenged.

SIX

At the end of January 1944, the 7118-ton tanker British Chivalry, lately out of dry-dock, lay at her berth in the South Australian port of Melbourne resplendent in a fresh coat of wartime grey. For a fifteen-year-old ship that had known nothing but hard voyaging all her life she looked in good shape. So thought her chief officer, Pierre Payne, as he surveyed the ship critically from the quayside. After three restful weeks in Melbourne, Bristol-born Payne, 29 years old, and with the horrors of the slaughter at Darwin long since relegated to the back of his mind, was in a mood to wax sentimental over his ship.

The British Chivalry had reached Melbourne early in the month with a full cargo of crude oil from Abadan, her bottom covered in barnacles, long grass growing on her waterline and with her hull running red rust. Much of this could be put down to the ravages of the past seven gruelling months. She had sailed from the Clyde in July 1943, experienced the horrors of the North Atlantic run for one voyage only, and was then sent around the Cape of Good hope to take her place on the monotonous shuttle service between Australia and the Persian

Gulf. Lack of time and opportunity for maintenance and the warm, fecund waters of the Indian Ocean had taken their toll. The long over-due dry-docking may have been prompted by the decrepit state in which the British Chivalry had been trailing her proud flag across the oceans, but more likely the Admiralty was concerned at her loss of speed and rising fuel consumption.

There had certainly been no complaints from the tanker's war-weary crew when faced with the unexpected bonus of three weeks in Melbourne. The southern summer was at its height and the lovely old city nestling at the head of Port Phillip Bay had a soft heart and an open hearth for the British seaman. At one time it seemed their stay would be even longer, for the famine in Iran was worsening and a plan was afoot to use the British Chivalry as a bulk grain carrier for one or more voyages. Fully loaded, she would have been able to lift in the region of 10,000 tons. Then it was realised that to put her sludge-coated cargo tanks in a fit state to carry grain would take the tanker out of service for an unacceptably long time. And so it was to be the usual compromise, a northbound passage in ballast, with 450 tons of bagged grain stowed in the small stores hold forward and in the summer tanks, which were rarely used for oil and required little cleaning.

The British Chivalry had also been selected to carry passengers to Abadan, but this was another plan that misfired. The four civilians, listed as employees of the Anglo-Persian Oil Company returning to the Gulf after leave in Australia, turned out to be two oilmen and their wives. The four were already on board when the Royal Navy stepped in, refusing permission for the women to sail, on the grounds that the dangers of the voyage were too great. The two husbands promptly walked down the gangway in the wake of their wives. In the weeks to come, Chief Officer Pierre Payne, for one, was to be eternally grateful to the Navy for refusing the women a passage.

At this stage of the war in the North Atlantic the U-boat menace was in decline, but there was a resurgence of German and Japanese submarine activity in the Indian Ocean. The demands of the Allied landings in Sicily and Italy had temporarily stripped Admiral Somerville's Eastern Fleet of many of its escort vessels, with dire results. Seven German and eight Japanese submarines were at large in the area and said to be roaming the shipping lanes with impunity. The Indian Ocean had suddenly become a high risk zone for the slow-moving merchant ship.

With a top speed of 10 knots – even with a clean bottom – the British Chivalry could be said to be in the above category. Owned by the British Tanker Company of London, she was a steamer built at Palmer's yard in Newcastle in 1929. In her day, long before an affluent world spawned the supertanker, she was considered to be of average size and carrying capacity. Her accommodation was neither luxurious nor sparse, her feeding sufficiently above the bare Board of Trade scale to be adequate, and when properly loaded or ballasted, she behaved tolerably well in a seaway. Her crew of 59, British but for a few exceptions – included 14 DEMS gunners, 9 from the Royal Navy and 5 of the Maritime Regiment.

On the morning of 1 February 1944, the British Chivalry steamed out of Melbourne harbour and entered the buoyed channel that leads across Port Phillip Bay to the open sea. On her forecastle head, Chief Officer Pierre Payne and the ship's carpenter, James McLenaghan, stood at anchor stations sniffing appreciatively at the clean, salt-laden air. It was a fine, sunny morning and both men, despite the good life they were leaving astern, were content to be once again heading out to sea. In terms of weather, the 30-day passage to the Gulf promised to be a pleasant one. After crossing the Great Australian Bight, quiescent at this time of the year but for the never-ending swell rolling up from the Roaring Forties, they would spend some days running before the blustery South-East Trades; the "soldier's wind" beloved by the old windjammer men. Once north of the Equator, the North-East Monsoon would prevail, bringing light, balmy winds and blue skies dotted with fair-weather cumulus. Payne glanced down at the ship's cat, contentedly rubbing against his leg. Having recently returned from yet another night out in Melbourne's dockland, the tom also appeared to sense good times ahead.

Looking beyond the coming sea passage, Payne speculated, idly, on the possibility of the British Chivalry returning to the UK from the Gulf. The war in the west was moving forward with great speed. Rommel had at last been cleared out of North Africa, Allied troops were advancing northwards in Italy and the Russians, aided by the awful severity of their winter, were throwing back the German panzers. There were also strong rumours of an impending return across the Channel to France. If and when this happened, vast quanties of oil would be required in Britain, and it was not beyond the bounds of possibility that the services of the British Chivalry would be urgently needed. After almost eight months away, Pierre Payne was feeling the pull of his home in Cardiff, where he had lived as an adopted Welshman for most of his life.

On the bridge of the tanker, Third Officer John Dahl's thoughts were running along similar lines. Dahl had escaped from his native Norway early in the war, leaving behind his mother and brother and sister. For Dahl the years of exile had been long and painful. As he stood beside the helmsman, with one eye on the compass and his ears cocked for the pilot's orders, he too debated the likelihood of an early return to Europe. When Allied troops went back across the Channel, he desperately wanted to be on hand. He had enjoyed the years spent at sea, was grateful for the friends he had made, but he was an architect by profession, a seaman by necessity. His work, his family and his country were calling him back.

Dahl stiffened instinctively as the British Chivalry's master, Captain Walter Hill, entered the wheelhouse. Here was a man who was even more of an enigma than Dahl himself. Captain Hill, 35 years old, was Belfast-born but an Eire national and a committed republican. He wore a gold shamrock on a chain around his neck, and although in command of a British ship, he made no secret of his dislike of his English cousins. For Walter Hill, the Battle of the Boyne had been fought only yesterday, but for all his prejudices, like so many of his countrymen, the twinkle in his eye and his ready laugh often excused his bigotry. He was also a first-class seaman, an attribute which, in the exacting environment of an ocean-going ship, compensates for a multitude of failings.

In the wireless room below the bridge, First Radio Officer C. Kennedy, a long way from his native Caithness, checked over his equipment preparatory to going to sea. The ancient spark-gap transmitter, the staccato crackle of which could be heard throughout the ship when in use, was a relic of a byegone age. Fortunately, Kennedy reassured himself, there should be no call to use the noisy contraption on the passage. While at sea, like all merchant ships in time of war, the British Chivalry would stay silent, her three radio officers keeping a listening watch around the clock. Only when instructed by the Admiralty, or in a case of dire emergency, would the transmitter be used. As his thoughts ran along these lines, Kennedy gave an involuntary shiver. He was a non-swimmer and loathe to dwell upon such things.

The six-day passage across the Great Australian Bight passed without incident. The benefits of the British Chivalry's recent dry-docking were evident; ballasted eight feet by the stern, she maintained a respectable 10 knots without effort. In these waters, there was little to fear from the enemy, and with the weather set fair, the days were used to good effect. For Pierre Payne, the ship already painted round by shore labour, this was a heaven-sent opportunity to tackle the more persistent areas of rust on deck, to oil and grease cargo gear, and to check safety equipment and lifeboats. This was also the time for the newly promoted boatswain, George Dunsby, whose predecessor had been landed sick in Melbourne, to prove his ability and establish his authority. Due to more illness, the deck crew he ran, had injected into it, a not altogether welcome, Australian element. Three of the new men, led by 30-year-old Able Seaman Harry Belcher of Melbourne, a typical hard-drinking Aussie, were having difficulty in coming to terms with the discipline of a British ship.

Cape Leeuwin, westernmost point of Australia, was rounded on 7 February and the British Chivalry settled down on a north-westerly course for the Persian Gulf. The long swell had lost much of its strength, and with the exception of the occasional lazy roll, the ballasted tanker forged ahead serenely. The warmth of the sun increased, giving rise to more activity on deck. Among those to be seen stripped to the waist were Gunlayer T. Beighton and Sergeant H. King, who, with their team of gunners, spent the days cleaning and exercising their guns. The British Chivalry's armament consisted of a 4-inch anti-submarine gun, a 12-pounder, a 120-mm, quick-firing Bofors, six Oerlikons and two twin .5-inch Colt machine guns. For a merchant ship the tanker was extremely well-armed, and given the opportunity, would be able to hit back hard at an attacking enemy. She was, however, without Asdic or depth charges, and therefore powerless to defend herself against a submerged submarine.

The fine weather continued, and aided by favourable currents, the British Chivalry's performance surprised even Chief Engineer W. Dickinson, who at 61 had given up a comfortable retirement to return to sea for the duration of the war. Despite steering a zig-zag course from dawn to dusk in accordance with Admiralty instructions, the ship was averaging 11 knots.

On the morning of the 15th, when 450 miles south-west of the Cocos & Keeling Islands, instructions were received from Perth to divert to the east of the planned route. This was the first indication that the enemy was active in the area. From then on there was an air of increased vigilance about the ship.

But the voyage progressed much as before, under untroubled skies and across a glassy sea, disturbed only by darting flying fish and shoals of playful dolphins. This was the stuff the cruise liner brochures are written around. Early on the 20th, the British Chivalry passed to the south of the Chargos Archipelago and altered her course to the north. She had roughly 2000 miles to go to reach the safety of the Persian Gulf, but she was now entering the area of greatest danger. She was at the confluence of the great shipping lanes from Africa, India and the Red Sea, where both German and Japanese submarines habitually lay in wait for their prey. Early on the 21st came the first sign that the Gods of War were abroad, when a distress call was heard from the Norwegian tanker Fenris, torpedoed 600 miles to the north.

Late that afternoon, Payne, who had the watch on the bridge, was surprised to hear the whine and crackle of the transmitter coming from the open door of the wireless room. He investigated and found Kennedy at the key, who explained that a shore station, believed to be Colombo, had requested the British Chivalry's present position, and that he was transmitting this, in code, on the orders of Captain Hill. Although he had no authority to countermand Hill's orders, Payne could not agree with this action. He felt the protective cloak of silence they had wrapped around themselves was being stripped away at a very dangerous time.

Payne's fears increased when Kennedy's transmission continued at intervals throughout the rest of the afternoon and into the evening. The senior radio officer was having great difficulty in passing his message. At ten o'clock that night, with the persistent crackle of the transmitter still resounding through the accommodation, Payne felt he must take action. Accompanied by Third Officer John Dahl, who had also become alarmed, the chief officer went to the wireless room. Kennedy, who was not at all happy with his lot, revealed his dilemma. Since the receipt of the message, purporting to have come from the C-in-C Colombo, he had been under orders from Captain Hill to pass the ship's position, no matter how long it took. And it was taking an interminably long time, for Colombo appeared unable to read Kennedy's transmissions and was monotonously asking for repeat after repeat. The radio officer now had serious doubts about the identity of the station he was in touch with.

To Pierre Payne, the whole thing stank of treachery. He suspected the tanker was being lured into a trap, duped into using her radio to provide a homing beacon for an enemy ship or submarine equipped with a W/T direction finder. John Dahl agreed with Payne's theory, and together the two officers called on Captain Hill to express their fears.

Hill was inclined to treat the matter lightly and accused Payne of overreacting because of past misfortunes associated with the month of February – Payne had lost his ship in the North Sea in February 1940, and again at Darwin in February 1942. The chief officer had no answer to this charge, but when Hill informed him that, in accordance with orders received from the C-in-C Colombo, he intended to cease zig-zagging at dawn next day, a bitter argument ensued. Payne was of the opinion that to dispense with the zig-zag would invite disaster, and said so forcibly. But, the power of the master of a merchant ship being what it is, Payne inevitably lost the argument.

When daylight came on the morning of the 22nd, it was with some misgiving that Pierre Payne, as officer of the watch, ordered the quartermaster at the wheel not to commence the usual daytime zig-zag. The sea was a flat calm and the visibility unlimited. The British

Chivalry, steering a straight and uninterrupted course, would present a target which not even a novice submariner could miss. And, unknown to Payne, just over that razor-sharp horizon waited a man, who was anything but a novice.

After an absence of nine months, Lieutenant Commander Nakagawa, ex-I-177, brutal destroyer of the hospital ship Centaur, was back at sea in a new and more powerful boat and eagerly searching for a kill. I-37, displacing 1,950 tons, carried a crew of 94, had a top surface speed of 24 knots, a range of 16,000 miles, and was armed with a 14-cm deck gun, a 20-mm anti-aircraft cannon, two heavy machine-guns, 17 torpedoes and a reconnaisance seaplane. Nakagawa was justifiably proud of his new command and intended to put her to good use. Whether he had any hand in the exchange of signals with the British Chivalry on the 21st is a matter for conjecture. It would have been a simple matter for I-37's W/T operator to impersonate Colombo, then feign poor reception and encourage Kennedy to keep repeating the coded position, thus enabling the submarine to home in on the unsuspecting tanker.

Breakfast in the officers' saloon of the British Chivalry on the morning of the 22nd should have been a hearty affair. The stores supplied in Melbourne were generous, and being mid-week, the menu featured a welcome treat of bacon, eggs and chips. Certainly, Pierre Payne, on the bridge since two hours before sunrise, was in a mood to indulge his appetite to the full. Unfortunately, when Captain Hill joined the table, all Payne's doubts about the wisdom of the wireless transmissions and the suspension of the precautionary zig-zag came welling up again. He could not resist expressing his fears to Hill, which led to another unpleasant argument. Payne was backed up by Chief Engineer Dickinson and Second Engineer Mann, who were also at the table, but Hill stubbornly insisted he was acting on orders from the Admiralty, orders he could not disobey. In the end, Payne stormed out of the saloon in a rage, leaving his mouth-watering breakfast to congeal on its plate. This was one action he was to bitterly regret in the days to come.

When he regained his composure, Payne went on deck, and accompanied by the boatswain, George Dunsby, made the rounds of the various maintenance and painting jobs in hand. This done, and having no pressing paperwork to attend to, Payne decided to assist Dunsby in cleaning out the cofferdam between the engine-room and the cargo tanks, where some sediment had been left by the Australian dockyard workers. It was the boatswain's intention to climb to the bottom of the cofferdam and use a hose to wash out the narrow compartment thoroughly, but Payne could not shake off the feeling that the ship was in grave danger. He insisted Dunsby wear a lifeline and would allow him to descend only a little way below deck level. This was not a very satisfactory arrangement, for the boatswain was forced to use one hand to hang onto the vertical ladder, while he played the hose with the other hand. Payne, crouched at the coaming of the cofferdam, tending the hose and lifeline.

On the bridge, the mounting tension was also evident. Third Officer John Dahl, having taken over the watch from Payne at 08.00, prowled uneasily from wing to wing, occasionally stopping to sweep the horizon with his binoculars. Under different circumstances the Norwegian would have considered it a privilege to be in charge of the bridge on such a morning. The sky was a faultless blue, the sea a sparkling millpond, on which the British Chivary's frothing wake stretched back, undeviating, as far as the eye could see. But Dahl, who shared Payne's fears for the safety of the ship, was uneasy.

Unknown to Dahl, his unease was fully justified. Five miles off the British Chivalry's starboard bow, I-37 was running submerged and manoeuvring into postion for the attack. Nakagawa's normally placid face was wreathed in smiles as he surveyed his quarry through the periscope. The unsuspecting tanker was holding a steady course to the north and taking no evasive action. She presented a perfect target.

It was 10.30, with the nose-twitching smell of freshly brewed coffee issuing from the officers' pantry when a shout from the gunner, on lookout in the starboard wing of the bridge, brought Dahl running through the wheelhouse. Following the man's outstretched arm, the third officer focussed his binoculars on a small disturbance in the water on the quarter. He, initially, thought the ripples were caused by the fin of a cruising shark, but then he caught the glint of the sun on glass, then the stick-like shape of a periscope. As the realisation dawned, Dahl saw the tracks of two torpedoes racing for the ship. He swung round, his voice rising to a high note as he roared at the helmsman.

The violent alteration of course Dahl ordered, came too late. One torpedo passed harmlessly astern of the British Chivalry as she swung in answer to the helm, but the other caught her square in the engine-room on the starboard side. A massive explosion followed, clouds of grey/black smoke billowed upwards from the open engine-room skylights, and the tanker slowed to a halt.

The approaching torpedoes had also been seen by the DEMS gunner on watch on the after gun platform, and it was his shout that alerted Payne at the top of cofferdam. The nightmare the chief officer had dreaded was upon them.

Payne's first concern was to bring the boatswain up on deck. George Dunsby was no lightweight, but with Payne hauling on the lifeline the boatswain reached the coaming of the cofferdam and flopped to the deck just as the second torpedo found its mark. Although deafened by the blast and showered with debris from the engine-room, only a few feet astern of where they were working, both men were unhurt.

Seconds after the explosion, Payne and Dunsby were joined by Captain Hill, who had come aft to ascertain the extent of the damage. The three men raced up the ladder to the poop and aft to the engine-room door. One quick glance below was enough to tell them the worst. The water was already over the top of the main engine, indicating the torpedo must have blasted a huge hole in the ship's side. There could be no hope for Fourth Engineer Morrison and the three firemen who had been on watch below.

Payne then remembered one of the jobs he had assigned to the apprentices that morning was to paint the after starboard lifeboat. He went up a deck and crossed to the starboard side. The boat had disappeared, and with it 17-year-old Apprentice Kenneth Bagshaw.

Hurrying to the other side of the boat deck, Payne discovered the port lifeboat was smashed, beyond all possible use. He rejoined the others, and as they returned forward along the catwalk, the sea was lapping over the bulwarks of the main deck. When they reached the lower bridge, they found the three radio officers attempting to break down the door of the wireless room. This had become jammed shut following the explosion, but as both main and emergency aerials were down, the efforts of the radio officers were pointless. No SOS would go out from the stricken tanker.

Captain Hill now gave the order to abandon ship in the two remaining lifeboats, which being stowed amidships beneath the bridge, had escaped damage. Payne made a dash for his cabin to collect his lifejacket and personal papers, before returning to the lower bridge to supervise the lowering of the port lifeboat. This boat was equipped with an engine, and despite the urgency of the situation, Payne took time to load extra tins of petrol from the nearby deck locker.

Although the men were outwardly calm, there was an understandable haste in their actions and Payne's boat was slightly damaged during lowering, but once in the water with its motor firing sweetly, it swept away from the ship's side. With Payne at the helm, they rounded the bow of the British Chivalry to meet up with the starboard boat, which was pulling away under oars. The two boats came together and a roll call was taken, revealing that Fourth Engineer S. Morrison, Apprentice K. Bagshaw, Chief Cook J. Sayers, and Firemen T. Byrne, J. Gallagher and R. O'Neil were missing. It was accepted that Morrison and the three firemen must have been killed in the engine-room and Bagshaw was probably blown over the side with the lifeboat he was working in. As the ship's galley was directly over the engine-room, it was presumed Sayers also lost his life when the torpedo struck.

There must always be casualties in war, and under the circumstances the British Chivalry had escaped lightly. Of her crew of 59, only 6 were dead, and although crammed into two boats, those who remained stood a good chance of survival. And there was another bonus. The tanker was heavily by the stern and her engines would never move again, but she was still afloat and could perhaps be re-boarded later. Then Nakagawa decided to finish the job he had begun.

On the orders of Captain Hill, Payne was using his motor boat to round up the four life rafts, released before abandoning ship, when the submarine came to the surface about a mile away. Her deck gun was manned as soon as her casings were clear and she opened fire. Whether by accident or design – Payne suspected the latter – the first half a dozen shells fell near the captain's boat, which was between the tanker and the submarine. Then the gunners concentrated on the British Chivalry. The shooting was poor, and it was not until the submarine closed to within 200 yards of the tanker that she began to register hits. Payne counted some 20 rounds fired, of which only three hit their target. The submarine then circled the ship and fired a torpedo at close range, which struck the British Chivalry in her port side amidships. This was too much for the gallant old tanker. Her stern submerged completely, her bows reared up, and she broke her back, sinking at 11.30, precisely one hour after she was first hit.

While Nakagawa was finishing off the British Chivalry, Payne continued to round up the drifting rafts. With the ship gone it was all the more urgent to collect the provisions and water stowed in the rafts. Although they were only 300 miles west of Adu Atoll, southernmost of the Maldives, where there was an RAF base, it could be many days, perhaps weeks before they were picked up.

It had not occurred to Payne there would be any more trouble from the enemy submarine. He assumed she was a German U-boat, and having sunk their ship, would do them no further harm; this being the Indian Ocean, it was unlikely the Germans would even bother to take prisoners. It was only when the submarine turned towards the lifeboats and opened fire on them with her 20-mm cannon that the awful realisation dawned. This was a Japanese submarine. The few gentlemanly laws of conduct still operable in this war did not apply.

Tearing his horrified eyes away from the advancing tracer, Payne shouted to his men to take cover in the bottom of the boat. Presently, he heard Captain Hill's voice, from the other boat, calling on him to semaphore to the submarine asking for a cease fire. To Payne, the idea seemed ludicrous; the cannon shells were thumping the water all around his boat – and in any case, how did one semaphore in Japanese? He experienced an insane desire to laugh, but he knew something had to be done quickly if they were not all to be killed. Summoning up his courage, he stood up and went through the motions of semaphoring the message, "What do you want us to do?" To his great amazement and relief, the firing stopped.

By this time the submarine had come to a halt close by, and men in her conning tower were signalling Payne to bring his boat alongside. He had little option but to obey, and his worst fears were confirmed as soon as the boat bumped alongside the rust-streaked, grey-painted hull. Men appeared on the casings dressed in khaki and wearing the shapeless peaked cap common to all the Japanese armed forces. In lisping pidgin English, one of them demanded that the captain identify himself. It took some time to explain to the Japanese that the captain was not in the boat. When this had finally been grasped, Payne was curtly ordered to tow the other lifeboat alongside.

Machine-guns mounted in the conning tower of I-37 were trained on Payne's boat, and he had no alternative but to cast off and carry out the order. Surprisingly, Walter Hill took the news calmly, for he must have known what the Japanese had in mind. Payne took the master's boat in tow and placed her alongside the submarine. He then backed away and lay-to 100 yards off. He watched Hill climb aboard, where he was saluted by the Japanese ratings lined up on the casing. The captain's lifeboat, now in the charge of 21-year-old Second Officer Richard Mountain, shipped oars and pulled away. When he was within shouting distance, Mountain informed Payne the Japanese had given orders for the two lifeboats to go in a westerly direction, with the motor boat towing the other. They had obviously seen the last of Captain Hill, and with the submarine's machine-guns trained on them, they were powerless to intercede on his behalf. It occurred to Payne that the Japanese were acting in a most civilised manner – totally at odds with their reputation – but he was not prepared to debate the issue. He passed a towrope to Mountain and the two boats set off to the west. At the same time, the submarine was seen to be moving away to the east.

The boats had not been under way for more than five minutes when they saw a man swimming towards them. Payne stopped the engine and a bedraggled John Dahl was hauled aboard. Believing the submarine to be German, and fearful that his family in Norway might suffer if he were taken prisoner, the third officer had taken to the water and hidden behind a raft, as soon as the enemy craft surfaced.

As Dahl stripped off his sodden clothes in the stern of Payne's boat, the bad dream suddenly became a nightmare. The alarm was given by George Dunsby, who was also in the stern of the boat, but facing aft. The boatswain's cry caused Payne, who had been questioning Dahl, to swing round. He saw that the Japanese submarine had reversed course and was coming towards them at speed. It was possible that the Japanese had decided to return Captain Hill to the boats, but Payne thought this very unlikely. He passed the word to the others, to be ready to go over the side.

Payne's suspicions were fully justified, for when she was about 30 yards off, the submarine opened fire with two machine-guns, the initial bursts being aimed at the second officer's boat. Payne and his crew, being prepared for the worst, took to the water and found cover on the far side of the boat. Those in Mountain's boat hesitated and then crouched down below the gunwales. The heavy bullets tore through the thin skin of their boat. The killing had begun.

Treading water near the stern of his boat, Payne witnessed the slaughter and was both sickened and angered. But he was given no time to dwell on the matter. The submarine was still coming in with her guns blazing. Alongside the machine-gunners in her conning tower, a man with a cine-camera could be seen calmly filming the attack. There followed a deliberate, cold-blooded attempt to destroy both the boats and the survivors, the submarine motoring back and forth only a few yards from the boats and opening fire each time she passed by. Payne and his men escaped by keeping their boat between them and the Japanese gunners. The same gunners were able to fire down on the men hugging the bottom of the other boat, killing or wounding most of them.

After an hour and a half of this macabre game of hide and seek, Payne concluded that the Japanese were determined not to leave one man of the British Chivalry's crew alive. It was a game the survivors in the water could not win, for sooner or later they would be caught without cover. He therefore passed the word for the men to clear away from the boat and feign death by drifting face down. This they did, but still the Japanese did not give up. As she cruised through the small groups of apparently lifeless bodies, I-37 deliberately slewed her stern from side to side in an effort to cut the helpless men to pieces with her twin propellors.

There followed a lull in the firing, and the submarine moved a short distance away. By now both lifeboats were badly holed and filling rapidly. Those still alive in Mountain's boat made the mistake of attempting to bail, and as they did so were cut down by a hail of bullets. Eventually, this boat badly damaged and full of bodies, sank, taking with it the portable lifeboat transmitter, and the last hope of communication with the outside world.

The killing ended as abruptly as it had begun. Nakagawa, satisfied that he had left no man alive, to tell of the sinking of the British Chivalry, ordered his gunners to cease fire and took I-37 away to the east. The time by George Dunsby's watch, the only serviceable timepiece remaining, was 14.00. Three and a half hours had passed since the torpedoing of the tanker, three and a half hours of terror that would live in the minds of those who survived, for the rest of their days.

When the submarine was safely over the horizon, Payne rallied the survivors and set about repairing the one lifeboat still afloat. With two men inside the boat to bail, the others worked underwater plugging the bullet holes with oakum and wooden plugs, stowed in the boat's locker for just such a contingency. It was dark before, having been plugged at least 17 holes, the boat was dry and could be boarded.

Only then, was Payne able to count the cost of the Japanese submarine's action. Surprisingly enough, it was not as bad as he had thought. In spite of Nakagawa's best efforts, only 13 had been killed and 5 injured. Amongst those who died in the machine-gunning were Chief Engineer Dickinson, Second Engineer Mann, First Radio Officer Kennedy, and the two senior DEMS men Gunlayer Beighton and Sergeant King. Of the injured, Chief Steward Cookesley and Able Seaman Morris were in a very serious condition. Even before Payne finished calling the role, Cookesley, a 56-year-old Cardiff man, died of his wounds and was buried near the spot where his ship had gone down.

Bearing in mind no SOS had been sent before the British Chivalry sank, Payne decided no purpose would be served by remaining where they were. But which way should they go? The nearest land, Adu Atoll, was 300 miles off, but the island was only a tiny speck on a vast ocean, requiring precision navigation, something Payne could not hope to offer. To go east would be to head towards Japanese occupied territory, an alternative no one wished to consider. Payne conferred with the other navigators, Mountain and Dahl, and it was agreed that, in view of the run of the current, the only feasible course was west-south-west towards the Seychelles. The distance was roughly 750 miles, a daunting undertaking in a leaking 24-ft lifeboat containing 39 men, some of them badly injured.

Having put the boat into a reasonably seaworthy condition, Payne now looked to the wounded. Able Seaman Morris, hit in the head and the right forearm by bullets, was in the most serious condition, lapsing from time to time into delirium. Seventeen-year-old Messroom Steward Taylor, had a gaping hole in his chest and a bullet lodged under his armpit, but would live. Noonan, the Australian pumpman had been shot in the throat and his windpipe was exposed, an injury that looked worse than it really was. Sloan, one of the Maritime

Regiment gunners, was also in a bad state, with a fearful shoulder wound, a bloody furrow across the front of his head and a hole in the back of his neck. Able Seaman Leslie Abbott, also a DEMS gunner, had a bullet lodged deep in his buttock.

The list of casualties would have daunted an experienced surgeon with all the resources of a well-equipped hospital at his disposal. Pierre Payne, on the other hand, possessed only a rudimentary knowledge of first aid, plus the lifeboat's rather basic medical kit. But, with the aid of Donkeyman Frank Alder, who also had some first aid training, he removed the bullet from Abbott's buttock and patched the others up as best he could, under the circumstances.

In settling the injured men it became quite plain the boat was hopelessly overcrowded and Payne therefore to transfer Second Officer Mountain with nine other men to one of the rafts. An effort was made to start the boat's engine, but this had been completely immersed in water, and despite the determined attentions of Third Engineer John Edwards, it would not fire. As there was not a breath of wind – they were in the Doldrums – and it was pointless to hoist the sails, the oars were shipped and they set off, rowing with the raft in tow. With those who were able taking turns at the oars, they rowed throughout that night and all next day. But by dusk on the 23rd it became all too clear they could not sustain such an effort for much longer. That night, the severely wounded Morris, who was on the raft, went mad and threw himself overboard. He was gone before the others had a chance to save him. Of the British Chivalry's company of 59 who had left Australia in such good spirits, only 38 now survived.

Following the death of Morris, Payne decided it would be wiser to bring all his men together in the boat, but first more room must be made. The only way to do this was to get rid of the now redundant engine, which occupied considerable space in the stern of the boat. The tools found in the boat locker, a few small spanners and a screwdriver, were totally inadequate for this job, but the incentive was great. At the cost of gallons of sweat and many badly bruised hands, the rusted holding-down bolts were finally unscrewed and the quarter-ton Thornycroft diesel lifted from its bed and manhandled over the side.

There was now much more space in the boat, which was taken up by the 10 men from the raft. Their additional weight reduced the freeboard of the boat to a mere ten inches, but Payne felt more at ease with all the men under his direct control. He was then able to turn his mind to the serious business of making a landfall. The boat was equipped with a compass and charts, and a sextant had been put on board before abandoning ship. With the help of Dunsby's watch, navigation should not prove too difficult. However, the Seychelles were 750 miles away, and should they miss these islands, the coast of Africa lay 1000 miles beyond that. The ordeal facing them would be no mean challenge, but they were in good spirits. Watches were set, those in the fore end of the boat keeping lookout, the men amidships manning the oars, while the three deck officers and three seamen in the stern attended to the steering. There could be no changing places for fear of swamping the boat. The wounded were laid on the bottom boards and covered by canvas awnings to protect them from the sun, which was high in the sky for much of the day and blazed down without mercy. Those at the oars in the waist of the boat suffered the worst agonies of thirst and sunburn. Fortunately, during the evening on the 25th a slight breeze sprang up and it was possible to hoist the sails. Conditions on board improved at once, for with the oars stowed out of the way on the thwarts, a protective canopy could be rigged over the midships section.

Although events had taken a turn for the better, Payne knew the wind was unpredictable and deemed it wise to plan for a voyage of at least 30 days. He accordingly instituted strict rationing of food and water, allowing each man three "meals" a day. Breakfast consisted of two malted milk tablets, one spoonful of pemmican and two ounces of water. At mid-day and in the evening, one malted milk tablet, one spoonful of pemmican, half a biscuit, one tablet of chocolate and 2œ ounces of water were handed out. It was a pitifully inadequate diet for grown men, made worse because many tins of provisons had been pierced by Japanese bullets and their contents saturated with salt water.

Drinking water was always going to be the greatest problem. A man can survive for weeks, even months, without food, he cannot hope to last more than a few days once his water runs out. It was, therefore, with some dismay that Payne viewed the cloudless skies overhead. They needed rain more than anything else, but as the days passed, the white-hot orb of the Equatorial sun continued to shine, uninterrupted by even a whisp of cloud. On the sixth day, after the sinking of the British Chivalry, despite Payne's careful rationing, the water in the wooden casks at the bottom of the boat was running dangerously low. And still the sky remained free of cloud. After a meagre breakfast, a general discussion took place on how they might eke out their last few pints of precious water. There was, of course, no easy solution, but the survivors showed, that even in such dire circumstances, the British seaman is capable of calling on a reserve of humour. The date was 1 March, St David's Day, and it was suggested, jokingly, the Welsh among them should try singing for rain. The only true Welshman in the boat was Third Engineer John Edwards, Cardiganshire born and reared, but Pierre Payne, having lived in Wales for most of his life, had come to regard himself as a native of the Principality. When prevailed upon, the two men stood up, bared their heads, and sang their national anthem in Welsh. The singing was not up to Cardiff Arms Park standard, for their lips were cracked and their throats dry, but the haunting strains of Mae Hen Wlad Nhadau – Land of my Fathers – floating on the still tropical air, brought tears to many eyes. It also brought much more in the way of moisture. No sooner had Payne and Edwards resumed their seats than the heavens opened and the boat was deluged with rain. The rain was so heavy and continuous the delighted survivors were able to drink their fill and replenish all the water casks, yet minutes before, there had not been a cloud in sight. To this day, Pierre Payne, a man not given to fanciful notions, will argue that miracles do sometimes happen.

St David's Day was the turning point in the fortunes of the survivors of the British Chivalry. They had broken out of the sultry Doldrums into an area of tropical rainstorms, and from then on they did not want for water. Each day they fixed the position of the boat, using the sextant and George Dunsby's watch, but progress was painfully slow. There were days when they appeared to be moving east instead of west, and in order to maintain morale, Payne took to falsifying the positions on the chart. Only Payne, Richard Mountain and John Dahl, being trained navigators, really knew what was happening. The lifeboat, sailing before light winds, was caught between the west-flowing Equatorial Current and a counter current running eastwards – and being carried along by whichever was predominant on the day.

The sea around the boat abounded with fish, including some very large and unwelcome sharks. A net was made and some of the smaller fish were caught, which, even when eaten raw, made a pleasant addition to the monotonous diet of lifeboat provisions. But, as day followed day with no end to the ordeal in sight, tempers became frayed and frequent arguments broke out in the crowded boat. The heavy rain squalls they had blessed, now became a curse, for with so little shelter the survivors were continually soaked to the skin. Their suffering was worse at night, when the cold seemed to penetrate deep into their bones. Salt water boils, swollen feet and legs, and, above all, the cramped conditions in the boat, made life a hell for those who were uninjured; for the wounded just staying alive was an intolerable burden.

Things came to a head one night, during a particularly fierce rain squall, when a fight broke out between two men, whose nerves had been stretched beyond breaking point. It took all the weight of Payne's authority to restore order, but when it was over, the mood in the boat remained ugly. It was not that the men concerned felt any real resentment towards each other, but they had begun to give up hope, and when hope goes, all is lost. Payne wondered how much longer he would be able to hold this band of battered, half-starved, but unquestionably brave men, together.

The answer to Payne's quandary was provided by Able Seaman Cleary, one of the DEMS gunners, an optician before the war and a quiet, unassuming man. Cleary suggested to Payne that a prayer might help, and, to his surprise the entire complement of the boat agreed.

Throughout time seamen have lived in conflict with the elements, often walking cheek by jowl with death on a daily basis, yet the majority do not express any strong religious beliefs. It is as though they feel their constant battle with nature is religion enough. On this occasion, the survivors of the British Chivalry obviously felt it was time to come to terms with God, and Payne, as the senior officer in the boat, was elected to lead them in prayer each day before breakfast. There was no bible or prayer book at hand, but Payne, drawing on the memories of his church-going youth, plus a certain amount of improvisation, contrived to hold a short and simple service each morning. The effect on morale was instant, and from then on the chief officer had no difficulty in holding the men together. This was just as well, for the boat was now making so little headway, Payne had privately given up hope of ever reaching land. Soon the food and water would run out and they would have to face a miserable death. He often thought it might have been kinder, if the Japanese had killed them all.

The 29th day of March, their thirty-seventh day in the boat, dawned fine and calm, without a cloud in the sky. The rains had been gone some time and Payne suspected they were drifting back into the Doldrums. The sun mounted the sky slowly, turning the boat into an open oven, packed with lolling humanity. Noon came again, and somehow the three navigators went through the farce of taking sights, for it must not be seen that they too had given up.

Later, during the heat of the afternoon, the ship's carpenter, Jim McLenaghan, and Able Seaman Arthur Light were squatting amidships, idling away the time with a pack of cards. Suddenly, McLenaghan, a phlegmatic Scot, who was facing aft, looked up and remarked casually that he could see a ship astern. Arthur Light, believing this to be a joke – and not in the best of taste – forcibly told the carpenter to save his twisted sense of humour for a more suitable occasion. But when McLenaghan persisted, Light finally glanced over his shoulder – pandemonium broke out. The ship, visible close astern, was no illusion.

Payne, who feared the boat might capsize, blew his whistle and restored order with difficulty. He had not yet seen the ship himself, but he put their much discussed plan into action. Oars were shipped, the sails lowered and smoke floats and distress rockets fired, each man carrying out his appointed task proficiently and without fuss – mentally, during the long lonely nights, they had rehearsed for this moment over and over again. However, the sea, having held them in its watery grip for 37 days, was not about to let go easily.

The British motor vessel Delane, on voyage from Calcutta to Cape Town, was passing through a known danger area, and when those on her bridge sighted the unidentified craft on the horizon, their suspicions were aroused at once. Captain King, who suspected the stranger might be an enemy submarine, ordered his crew to action stations and rang for emergency full speed. He intended to adopt the recommended procedure for a merchant ship faced by an enemy submarine – to turn stern-on and run away, at the same time opening fire with the 4.7-inch the Delane mounted on her poop but, as so often happens with a motor vessel of her type, when the Delane's engine was given the extra boost of fuel, it stopped dead. That left the ship drifting, beam-on, to the suspected U-boat with her gun manned and ready to fire. At that moment her chief officer, who had personal experience of being adrift in a lifeboat, appeared on the bridge and recognised the lifeboat for what it was. Captain King was persuaded to hold his fire and a tragedy was averted. The British Chivalry's survivors, who had endured so much for so long, had come within an ace of being destroyed by their own kind.

When Pierre Payne and his men reached the deck of the Delane, they presented a pitiful sight. Their eyes still held a spark of life, but they had only just enough strength to haul their emaciated bodies, hung around with salt-caked rags, over the bulwarks of the British ship. It must have been an even more strange and moving sight to see these stumbling scarecrows, led by Chief Officer Pierre Payne, go down on their knees and offer prayers for their deliverance.

The British Chivalry's survivors were picked up in 04° 55'S 65° 32'E, some 720 miles to the east of Payne's dead reckoning position. Although they had been steering in a westerly direction, the course made good was south-south-west, and the distance 320 miles. They had, in fact, been drifting in a southerly direction at an average of 8œ miles a day. Had they not, quite by chance, been found by the Delane, another thousand miles of empty ocean stretched ahead of them before they either fetched up on the shores of Mauritius or Reunion, or sailed on to Antartica. On the basis of their previous rate of drift, to have reached the islands alone would have taken them another four months. It is doubtful if any could have survived.

Captain Walter Hill, who was forced to stand on the deck of I-37 and watch the brutal machine-gunning of his men, went through a lonely ordeal of his own. On the voyage back to Penang, during which he was a silent witness to more atrocities committed by Nakagawa, he stubbornly refused to answer questions put to him by the Japanese and was periodically taken out on deck, blindfolded, with his hands tied behind his back. The implied threat was that he would be thrown to the sharks, but the Irishman would not to give in. On arrival at Penang, Hill was put on a starvation diet for "daring to take up arms against the Emperor." He was released when Japan fell to the Allies but, for some reason, declined to give evidence against his captors to the War Crimes Commission.

SEVEN

Following its crushing defeat at the hands of the Americans off Midway and the premature death of Admiral Yamamoto, the Japanese surface fleet was reluctant to venture back into the Indian Ocean again. However, the chain of sinkings set in motion by Admiral Nagumo, with the Easter Sunday annihilation of the British Eastern Fleet in 1942, had continued in the capable hands of a force of seven German and eight Japanese submarines. Working independently and virtually unhindered by any opposing forces, these wily predators roamed the shipping lanes, inflicting consistent heavy losses on Allied merchant ships, most of whom were sailing alone and unprotected.

When, in September 1943, the British Eastern Fleet returned from Mombasa to Colombo, it was hoped there would be a change for the better. But Admiral Somerville had under his command only one ancient battleship and nine cruisers, five of which were of pensionable age. The fleet had no aircraft carriers, and as far as convoy escort work was concerned, this was in the hands of a few armed merchant cruisers; ageing passenger liners that had once plied these same trade routes in peacetime. There could be no question of escorting all merchant shipping. Convoys were introduced on the routes considered to be most vulnerable, mainly those between the Gulf of Aden and the west coast of India and Ceylon, with a dramatic fall in the number of sinkings, but it was not long before the Admiralty was grumbling about "unacceptable delays"; the assembly and shepherding of merchant ships into convoys, played havoc with their schedules. Fortunately, the German U-boats appeared to be gradually withdrawing from the Indian Ocean, and towards the end of 1943 it was possible to discontinue convoys, except for troopships and others at great risk.

It was around this time that U-188, commanded by Kapitan-Leutnant Siegfried Ludden, appeared on the scene. She was one of three survivors of a group of nine U-boats which left Lorient for the Indian Ocean earlier in the year. Four of their number were sunk by Allied aircraft as they were crossing the Bay of Biscay, and two more lost, again to air patrols, to the north of Madagascar. Siegfried Ludden, having seen service with the North Atlantic wolf packs, was a commander of considerable experience, and this no doubt stood him in good stead during the three-month-long, hazardous voyage around the Cape of Good Hope. But U-188 then spent a largely fruitless two months haunting the upper reaches of the Mozambique Channel. Admiral Somerville's convoys, although lightly escorted, were well organised, and unlike in the North Atlantic, Ludden did not have the weather on his side. Then, coincident with the suspension of the convoys, U-188 moved north to take up station to the east of Socotra. This lonely, forbidding island, which stands sentinel off the eastern entrance to the Gulf of Aden, marks one of the vital crossroads of the Indian Ocean. Through this focal point, in war and in peace, must pass all ships plying between Europe and India, whether sailing via the Cape or Suez. It was here Ludden lay in wait for ships now proceeding independently, and experienced an immediate change of luck.

From 20 January to 9 February 1944, U-188 sank no fewer than seven Allied merchant ships of 42,549 tons.

Ludden's sudden successes sent the Admiralty into an understandable panic and convoys were at once reinstated on the Gulf of Aden – Bombay/Colombo routes. It was thus that the 5189-ton British motor vessel Sutlej found herself leaving Aden, in convoy, on 15 February. Although bound for Fremantle, she was obliged to sail far out into the Arabian Sea in company with a number of ships heading for Bombay, before she would be free to go south.

Built in Glasgow in 1940 and owned by James Nourse & Company, a subsidiary of the prestigious P & O Line, the Sutlej sailed from Birkenhead in late December 1943, and following the discharge of her outward cargo, loaded 9,700 tons of rock phosphates in the Red Sea port of Kosseir. Her master, 37-year-old Captain Dennis Jones of Bath, although taking some comfort from the protection provided by the convoy, did not welcome the extra 1000 miles added to his passage by this precautionary measure. It would result in, at the very least, another four days added to the long run down the Indian Ocean; four days extra fuel burned and four more days exposed to the stalking enemy. It was the latter that caused Jones the most concern, for the Sutlej's cargo of phosphates lay heavy in the bottom of her holds, a deadweight which would drag her down within minutes if she were torpedoed. Although such things were never discussed, except jokingly, Captain Jones's concern was shared by his crew, to a man. Lifejackets were always kept close at hand, on or off watch.

The Sutlej, named for a Punjabi river that rises in the foothills of the Himalayas, carried a crew of 73, made up of 9 British officers, 51 Indian ratings, a Chinese carpenter and 9 DEMS gunners. Her defensive armament comprised a 4-inch, a 12-pounder, four Oerlikons, two twin Marlins, and various rockets designed to bring down low-flying aircraft, a foe she was unlikely to meet in these waters. Her life-saving equipment was also of the usual wartime standard. She had lost one of her four life rafts overboard during a gale in the Atlantic on the outward passage, but her four lifeboats and three remaining rafts were adequate for the number of crew.

On 20 February, at a point mid-way across the Arabian Sea, the Sutlej took her leave of the convoy and turned south. For the next 1500 miles she would have, to the west of her, the thousand and one tiny islands and reefs that make up the archipelagoes of the Lacadives, the Maldives and Chargos, a long chain of coral islands reaching down to 7 degrees south of the Equator. This would be the most dangerous leg of the passage, and Captain Jones was anxious to put it behind him without delay. It needed only a word with the Sutlej's chief engineer, 31-year-old Welshman Richard Rees, and the ship was soon making her maximum 10 knots, her blunt bows carving a zig-zag path through a flat calm sea of the purest blue. Once clear of Diego Garcia, the course lay south-east for 2,900 miles across open sea to Australia's west coast. Jones expected to reach Fremantle on about 10 March, three months out of Birkenhead.

When, at 10.30 on the morning of the 22nd, the British Chivalry was torpedoed, the Sutlej was only 500 miles to the north of her position, but those on board the Nourse Line ship had no inkling of the carnage taking place over the horizon. If the tanker's wireless room had not been wrecked, events might have taken a very different turn for the Sutlej.

The crossing of the Equator on the evening of the 23rd went almost unnoticed, for the traditional visit of Neptune and his handmaidens had been suspended for the duration of the war. Thus 16-year-old Third Radio Officer Harry Robinson missed his first, and as it would transpire, only, chance of gaining the coveted Crossing the Line certificate. The morning of the 24th dawned fine and clear with the promise of yet another scorching day. There was a flurry of excitement in the forenoon, when the Sutlej overtook two Arab dhows running before the light north-easterly breeze. On the bridge the officer of the watch, Third Officer Frank Newell, a 25-year-old Londoner, examined the graceful craft through his binoculars and marvelled at the navigational prowess of these dark-skinned men who sailed this lonely ocean without compass or chart.

At 18.15 on the evening of the 26th, the Sutlej had reached latitude 9 degrees South, 190 miles south-west of Diego Garcia, and was continuing to make good progress. A day or two more and she would be out of the danger area. It was a fine, peaceful evening, with the setting sun turning the western horizon to a sea of beaten copper. Dinner being over Chief Engineer Richard Rees took to the boat deck to stretch his legs before the darkness closed in. At 31 – very young for his rank – Rees was enough of a romantic to appreciate the sheer beauty of the tranquil scene. As he walked and took deep breaths of the clean, salty air, he concluded it must have been on such an evening as this, that the mythical call of the sea was born.

Chief Officer Edwin Quick, a Cornishman of 39, on watch on the bridge at the time, viewed the end of the day with a more practical eye. It would soon be time to take up his sextant and search for the first stars appearing in the gathering twilight. The ship was near the alteration point for the long south-easterly leg to Fremantle, and an accurate position was needed before changing course. In the opposite wing of the bridge, Captain Dennis Jones rested his arms on the smooth varnishwork of the taffrail and gazed out to sea; for him darkness could not come soon enough. There would be no moon this night, and with cloud building up to the east, the Sutlej should soon be hidden from the prying eyes of the enemy. Jones savoured the prospect of, at long last, being able to sleep easy in his bunk.

In the officers' dining saloon the tables had been cleared and three men were playing cards. Frank Newell had another hour and a half to

kill before taking up his watch on the bridge, while the other partici-
pants in the game, Second Officer Alexander Chisholm and Second
Radio Officer John Whittaker, both due on watch at midnight, would
soon be leaving to go to their bunks. It was a Saturday evening and the
talk was inevitably of the good fortunes of those at home, downing
their pints in the pubs of Liverpool, London and Glasgow. The mood
in the saloon was subdued, the conversation muted, for the players,
like Captain Jones, were waiting for the safety curtain of the night to
descend.

At 18.20, the sun sank below the horizon and the short tropical
twilight set in, accompanied by the rumble of distant thunder. Dark
rain clouds could be seen massing to the east. As per standard proce-
dure, the zig-zag was discontinued for the night and the Sutlej settled
down on a steady course. Richard Rees, tirelessly pacing the port side
of the boat deck, glanced at the clouds gathering to port and decided
it was time to return to the good book, waiting in his cabin. He was
about to enter the accommodation when he caught sight of a long,
feathered track, racing towards the ship. As he watched dumbstruck,
he was conscious of the Sutlej leaning gently to port as the helm went
hard to starboard. The bridge had seen the torpedo and was taking
desperate avoiding action.

But the British merchantman was no sleek-hulled destroyer able to
execute tight emergency turns. She responded to her helm as best she
could, but the Japanese torpedo slammed into her port side, striking
between her No.1 and 2 holds. The half-ton warhead exploded with a
deafening roar, ripping open the hull and sending a column of water,
debris and dust to the height of the masthead. Nakagawa's I-37, after
laying in wait for four days, had found her next victim.

Dense clouds of smoke and dust enveloped the fore part of the ship
and Rees was unable to see the extent of the damage, but the Sutlej
was tipping by the head and the strident clamour of alarm bells was

loud on the night air. His first thought being for his men on watch below, he made a dash for the ladder at the after end of the deck. By the time he reached the engine-room door, the engines had stopped and he was relieved to see Fifth Engineer John Waters, accompanied by his donkeyman, greaser and fireman of the watch, appear on deck, unscathed.

Rees's next concern was for his own life. Running forward to his cabin for his lifejacket, he then set off for his boat station on the starboard side of the bridge. He had not gone more than a few yards when he found himself up to his waist in water. The Sutlej was settling rapidly by the bows and her decks were already awash forward of the funnel. The ship was sinking under him. With his heart thudding, Rees turned back and took the ladder to the boat deck at a run.

On the boat deck Rees met Second Officer Chisholm and Third Engineer Arthur Bennett, whom he joined in an attempt to lower the port lifeboat. But time was running out. The stern of the Sutlej had risen high in the air, and realising she was about to take her last plunge, Rees shouted to the others to leave the boat and follow him overboard.

Still deafened from the crash of the torpedo, Third Officer Frank Newell was hard on the heels of his fellow card players as they spilled out of the saloon. His cabin was close by and he wasted a few precious moments in collecting his lifejacket and canvas bag containing his personal papers and valuables, before making a dash for his lifeboat on the port side of the lower bridge. The deck was deserted and the boat hung bow-down from its davits, held only by the after falls, probably as a result of the explosion. A quick glance forward showed the forecastle head already under water. The Sutlej was going fast. Newell hurled his precious canvas bag into the boat and climbed after it, hoping to free the after tackle when the boat hit the water. As he was struggling with the heavy block, the sea washed over him and he felt himself being sucked down into the darkness.

The Sutlej took just under four minutes to sink, dragged under by the sheer weight of her cargo of phosphates. When Richard Rees came to the surface, he found himself treading water alongside Arthur Bennett. Of Chisholm and the lifeboat they had tried unsuccessfully, to launch, there was no sight. To compound an already bad situation, darkness had fallen. Fortunately, a dark shape floating by turned out to be the raft used for painting the ship's hull when in port. It was a crude affair, consisting of four 40-gallon drums lashed together within a wooden framework, but the two men, still dazed by their traumatic experience, hauled themselves aboard, joining an Indian fireman, who had preceeded them by a few minutes.

Standing erect on the swaying raft Rees looked around at the depressing scene. The sea was covered with wreckage marking the last resting place of the Sutlej; broken hatchboards, strips of tarpaulin, planks of scorched dunnage wood from the holds, and an upturned lifeboat. In the midst of this pitiful flotsam, dozens of lifejacket lights bobbed, rhythmically, as though performing a grotesque torchlit ballet. Although the Sutlej had gone down with a rush, it seemed a large number of her crew had survived. It was also fortunate that the ship's fuel tanks did not appear to have ruptured, for there was no clinging black oil on the water. Rees and Bennett began to haul as many men on board their small raft as it would safely hold.

A few minutes later the engineers' rescue work was interrupted when I-37 surfaced and began to play her searchlight over the sad wreckage she had created. The raft was caught in the beam and Rees watched, with a sinking feeling in the pit of his stomach, as the submarine moved closer, its long, dark shape like some primeval monster sliding over the surface of the sea towards them.

The raft bumped against the hull of the submarine and a line was thrown, which Bennett made fast. Then the questioning began, a disembodied voice from the direction of the conning tower demanded to know the whereabouts of the master. Rees answered, quite truthfully, that he believed Captain Jones had gone down with the ship. He had established Jones was last seen, entering the wireless room. Seemingly satisfied with Rees' answer, the sing-song voice went on to ask the routine questions regarding the ship's name, her cargo and destination. Rees could now make out a machine-gun trained on the raft from the conning tower and had little alternative but to give the required information. In any case, he reasoned, with the Sutlej lying several thousand fathoms deep, it was hardly worth risking martyrdom.

Satisfied he had gleaned all the information he was likely to get from this pathetic band of half-drowned survivors, Nakagawa ordered the raft to be cast off and then tried to ram it. Fortunately for Rees and his companions, the bow wave of the submarine shouldered the raft aside and only slight damage was sustained. Rees hoped this might be the end of the matter, but he had not reckoned with I-37's machine-gunners, who were under orders to finish the job. They opened fire on the raft, spraying it liberally, but their aim was poor and no one was hit. The men in the water, on the other hand, provided targets that could hardly be missed. From his vantage point on the raft Rees watched, sickened, as the heavy bullets thudded into the helpless men.

Over the next hour, Nakagawa systematically quartered the area, using his machine-guns to good effect whenever a target presented itself. When I-37 finally motored away, Richard Rees and Arthur Bennett, appalled by the slaughter they had been forced to witness, looked around for the living. Soon there were twelve men clinging to the raft, including Second Engineer George Turner and Chief Cook

Johar Biswao. Unfortunately, the Indian died of his wounds shortly after being picked up.

The auxiliary raft was too small to support eleven men for long, so it was decided to hunt for the upturned lifeboat, seen amongst the wreckage earlier. But the overloaded raft was difficult to manoeuvre, and as it was now completely dark, a thorough search of the area was impossible. It was only by chance they stumbled upon two of the Sutlej's large life rafts, drifting, lashed together. On board were Fourth Engineer James Fitzpatrick, Able Seaman Robert Houghton, one of the ship's DEMS gunners, the Indian purser V.M. Josephs, the Chinese carpenter and seven Indian ratings. As would be expected, they were all in a thoroughly wretched state, having endured not only the sinking but interrogation and ramming by Nakagawa. Rees, as the senior officer present, took charge and distributed the 22 survivors equally between the two larger rafts, each of which measured 15 ft by 8 ft, leaving the small raft to drift on the end of a towline. They made themselves as comfortable as possible and waited for daylight to come.

Frank Newell was alone when he came to the surface, after breaking free from the suction of the sinking ship. All around him floated the shattered debris of what had once been his temporary home and place of work. The darkness, the complete absence of other survivors, and the sudden desperate realisation his plight had brought Newell near to panic, when he sighted the upturned lifeboat. It was not more than 30 feet away from him but to reach it he had to abandon his life-jacket. Clinging to the keel of the boat he found three Indian ratings, who were hysterical and offered him no assistance. Newell hauled himself up onto the keel, with difficulty, and once aboard was violently sick, bringing up all the sea water he had swallowed. He lay quiet for a while, regaining his strength, and as he did so he heard the sound of diesel engines near by and a voice calling for the Sutlej's captain and chief engineer to give themselves up. Nakagawa was still looking for prisoners. The submarine passed close by, but either the Japanese had not seen the upturned boat, or they declined to bother with it.

Almost as though they had been waiting for the Sutlej's end to be made final, the clouds which had been building up in the east now moved in and rain fell in torrents, continuing, unabated, throughout the rest of the night. Rees and his men, aboard the two rafts, spent a miserable night, cold, wet and wracked by sea sickness. When daylight came at last, the sea was devoid of wreckage, but they caught sight of more survivors on what appeared to be another raft, drifting about one mile off. Rees rallied his men and strenuous efforts were made to paddle across the intervening stretch of water, but they could make little progress. The rafts were too heavy, and the men too exhausted to close the gap.

The "raft" sighted by Rees was in fact the Sutlej's lifeboat. During the night, Frank Newell had picked up two more Indian crew members, and as soon as the submarine was out of sight, the six men righted the boat, by hauling on the bilge keel, until it rolled over and was floating upright on its buoyancy tanks. Much of the gear, including most of the oars, had gone, but the hull of the boat was intact. Bailing out, while lashed by heavy rain squalls, was a wretched, back-breaking job, but the men set-to with a will. By midnight the boat was as dry as it ever would be. A few minutes later, a shout was heard and a baulk of timber, bearing Gunner Holgate, one of the Sutlej's four Maritime Regiment gunners, appeared out of the darkness. Holgate was dragged over the gunwales, making the total complement in the boat up to seven, two Europeans and five Indians. When the two rafts were spotted at daylight, Newell hoisted the sail, but the wind had fallen away and his efforts to join up with Rees were in vain.

After riding to a sea anchor for much of the day, Rees gave up hope of reaching the other survivors and decided he must concentrate on saving the men to whom he was immediately responsible. The prospects were not good. The Sutlej had gone down so quickly it seemed unlikely that an SOS had gone out. The absence of any searching aircraft seemed to confirm this. Rees was left with no alternative but to make for the land, this, for an engineer with no knowledge of navigation, in charge of two cumbersome rafts, with the sailing qualities of waterlogged beer crates, was an almost impossible assignment. The nearest inhabited land, the island of Diego Garcia some 190 miles to the north-east, was only 15 miles by 1œ miles and 23 feet above sea level at its highest point – a mere speck of coral on this great ocean. The odds against making such a difficult landfall were astronomical, but Rees knew he must try if they were not to die a lonely and pointless death.

Having emptied the small raft of its provisions and water, it was cut adrift, for it would be more of a hindrance than a help. The square sails of the larger rafts were now hoisted optimistically, but without wind they were completely at the mercy of the current, which Rees fervently hoped would take them north-east.

The rafts carried the usual provisions, in the form of biscuits, pemmican and malted milk tablets, plus 50 gallons of fresh water. The water, if carefully rationed, would last the 22 men about two months, while the food could possibly supplemented by catching fish. As it turned out, in the weeks that followed, rain fell at frequent intervals, and they were never short of water, while the sea around the rafts teemed with small fish. It was left to the Europeans to catch the fish, for the Indians had lapsed into a state of total apathy, but the harvest proved to be disappointing, until Rees turned his engineering skills to fashioning a harpoon. This, in the hands of First Tindle Shahib Sadick Sardor, who had learned the art of spearing fish as a boy in India, soon began to provide a regular supply of fresh food. Sea birds also took to circling the rafts, and an Indian steward, Fazle Hug Mangloo, showed an unexpected flair, catching them with his bare hands whenever they landed on the raft's canvas awning. A stove was made from an empty biscuit tin, and using a second tin as a pot, birds and fish were cooked over a fire kindled from planks of wood, stripped from the small abandoned raft. The hot, fresh food worked wonders, producing a feeling of well-being amongst the survivors that lasted for some days.

On 17 March, the twentieth day adrift, two small islands were sighted, but a wind persistently blowing offshore defeated all efforts to beach the rafts. Flares were burned at night, but no answering signals were seen, leading Rees to believe the islands were uninhabited. It is possible the rafts were off the southern tip of Diego Garcia, the low-lying land and clumps of palm trees giving the appearance of two islands at a distance. The only habitation on Diego Garcia, the RAF base, was on the north-west corner of the island, from which the survivors flares may not have been visible. When, at last, the land faded from sight, a cloud of depression descended. Some of the Indians, whose natural instinct was to lie down and fatalistically await death, became surly and quarrelsome.

On 27 March, after thirty days of this aimless drifting, Rees made the decision to split the two rafts, working on the theory that this would increase their chances of being sighted by passing ships or aircraft. It was a difficult decision, for there is always comfort in numbers, but a logical tone. George Turner and James Fitzpatrick, the two Europeans on the other raft, agreed, and the ropes which had been holding the two together, were cast off. By daybreak they had lost sight of each other.

HMS Flamingo rescuing survivors of Sutlej

Sixteen more days passed, with the sky and sea as empty as they had been since I-37 motored away, leaving them to their fate. Most of the Indians had given up the will to live, and even Richard Rees and his two European companions, Bennett and Houghton, had begun to despair. Then, in the early hours of the morning of 12 April, when hope was at a very low ebb, the lights of a ship were seen on the horizon. Flares were burned and the ship headed towards the raft, but she passed by at a distance of about 4 miles giving no sign of having seen the distress flares. Rees concluded she must be a neutral, afraid to approach lest she run into a trap. The long ordeal looked set to continue.

Next morning, the raft was surrounded by sharks, ominously circling and waiting. The morale of those on board plunged into a bottomless abyss. Then, when the merciless sun once again neared its zenith, the silent prayers of the night were answered. A Catalina – in response to a report by the unknown ship – flew overhead, swooped low and dropped a package, which landed in the water some thirty yards away. Defying the sharks, Arthur Bennett and Fazle Hug Mangloo plunged overboard and swam to the floating package, Bennett, who was very weak, ran into difficulties on his way back and Mangloo, courageously, went to his assistance. However, both men regained the raft, bringing with them the package, which contained some very welcome provisions.

From then on events moved rapidly. On the following morning, another Catalina came over, failing to locate the raft, until Rees decided to use the last remaining distress flare in the locker. At 16.30 the survivors knew their ordeal was over, when a mast and funnel came over the horizon, and the sloop HMS Flamingo bore down on them. In response to a message from the first Catalina, Flamingo had steamed at full speed, 430 miles, from Adu Atoll, where she was based. She had, on board, the survivors from the other raft, picked up two hours earlier and only 25 miles away. When sighted, the two rafts had been adrift for almost seven weeks and had covered 650 miles to the north-east. They were caught in the Equatorial Counter Current, which, would have borne them relentlessly across the Indian Ocean, to cast them ashore, months later, somewhere on the west coast of Sumatra. Of Richard Rees and his men only a few blackened, sun-dried corpses would have remained.

HMS Flamingo approaches one of Sutlej's life rafts

Following his unsuccessful bid to join up with the rafts, Frank Newell decided his best course of action was to sail the boat towards the nearest large land mass, Madagascar. The distance was immense, over 1200 miles, but the boat would run before the prevailing north-easterly wind, and, in a day or two, come under the influence of the westerly flowing Equatorial Current. He had charts and a compass and the boat was well stocked with fresh water and provisions, more than enough to sustain seven men on a very long voyage. At noon on 27 February, the sails were hoisted and the boat set off on a WSW'ly course. Newell was hoping to make the British naval base at Diego Suarez, at the northern end of Madagascar.

Newell's main problem was not of a physical nature. He was unfortunate enough to have, on board, the Sutlej's deck serang, Jabal Hug, who from the outset challenged the third officer's authority. Under Hug's leadership, the other Indians became thoroughly uncooperative, almost belligerent. Newell received some support from Gunner Holgate, the only other European in the boat, but for much of the time he was fighting a lone battle, steering the boat, navigating, handing out rations, and even keeping guard over the stores at night, to prevent the Indians helping themselves.

Survivors of Sutlej on Adu Atoll. Chief Eng.
Richard Rees, second from left

The voyage was long and painful, with a constant battle for supremacy raging between Newell and Hug. Apathy was rife and arguments frequent. On one occasion, the serang attempted to murder Holgate with an axe after a quarrel over the rations, the gunner was saved, only by the intervention of Newell.

The wind held steady in the north-east, but freshened as they moved south, building up a rough following sea. On 29 March, while Newell continued his lone vigil at the tiller and his crew languished in the shelter of the side screens, disaster struck. The boat gybed, and caught square on the beam by a heavy sea, overturned, throwing its occupants into the water. The Indians, led by the militant Jabal Hug, were all for leaving the boat as it was and riding on the keel, as they had been doing when Newell first found them, but the plucky third officer would not tolerate such suicidal apathy. However, it took twenty-four hours of cajoling, threatening, and in the end, bribing, with the promise of extra rations, to get the boat righted and bailed out.

When the boat was finally rolled over, it was found the damage was serious. The mast had snapped off at gunwale level, and the mainsail was missing, as was much of the boat's small gear, including the vital compass and charts. This was sufficient to cast an even deeper air of despondency over the boat, and it was left to Newell to rig a sea anchor so they could safely ride head to the wind and sea for the rest of the day and night. Next morning, again without help from the others, Newell rigged a jury mast and sail, using an oar and a canvas side screen. The boat limped on, with Newell and Holgate sharing the watches at the tiller and steering by the sun and the stars.

Early on the morning of 2 April, 58-year-old Amir Hussain, one of the Sutlej's quartermasters, died, occasioning a further drop in morale. Had it not been for the determination of Frank Newell, all hope of survival would have been abandoned there and then, but the young Londoner, having come thus far, was determined to reach land.

On the fortieth day adrift, came the first sign that they were not, after all, completely alone on this wide, tossing ocean, when an electric light bulb floated by. It was a tiny, insignificant thing, probably thrown overboard from a ship, but it was a symbol of hope for Newall. Next morning, 7 April, the young third officer's courage and perseverance was at last rewarded, when a smudge of cloud on the horizon hardened into land. For the rest of that day and well into the night, they sailed towards land, Newell calling a halt after midnight, for they were sailing into the unknown. At daylight, they set off again, and were within 10 miles of the shore, when picked up by HMS Solvra at 08.00.

When the six survivors boarded HMS Solvra, they found they were off the coast of Madagascar, only 90 miles south of Diego Suarez, the very point Newell had been aiming for. So ended a magnificent feat of open boat navigation – probably one of the finest ever recorded. Sailing virtually single-handed, the 25-year-old officer had covered 1300 miles in 41 days. His lifeboat had been twice capsized, dismasted, and without compass or charts for the final ten days of the voyage, while his crew had been, at best uncooperative, at worst downright obstructive. That any of them survived at all, was due, purely, to the efforts of Frank Newell. The Naval Officer in Command at Diego Suarez told the Admiralty: Frank Leslie Newell, the third officer, has been living in the wardroom of the Naval Base since his arrival at Diego Suarez. He has created an excellent impression by his modest demeanour, sober habits and general attitude, after having gone through what must have been a great ordeal, in which he showed resourcefulness, skill and courage of a very high order. Nakagawa's work on the night of 26 February, was yet another example of the depths of bestiality, to which he was prone to descend. His torpedo and machine-guns had taken the lives of 43 innocent men, and 2 more were to die later as a direct result of his actions.

EIGHT

One hundred and fifty years of British rule had welded India, a country of 300 million inhabitants, having 200 diverse tongues and 1000 incompatible religions, into a land of comparative order and stability. But, any unity achieved was lost, when the Japanese armies rampaged across the Pacific and into South-East Asia. The fiasco of Pearl Harbor, the pathetic surrender of Singapore and the swift collapse of the Dutch East Indies, destroyed for ever, the myth of white supremacy. Then, as the Japanese advanced westwards, India moved quickly towards internal strife. The main political faction in the subcontinent, led by Mahatma Gandhi, urged that India declare neutrality in the war, while powerful extremist groups favoured joining forces with the Japanese, to oust the British once and for all. Open revolution was never far below the surface.

Burma fell in March 1942, and for the first time in the history of the Raj, India was threatened with invasion by a foreign power. Total political chaos was avoided, only by the timely occurrence of another of the country's periodic famines. This one was exacerbated by the abrupt suspension of supplies of rice from Burma, and a huge influx of refugees from the same source. Once again, the responsibility for filling empty bellies fell on the despised British who, in turn, looked to the swollen granaries of Australia for immediate help.

When, in late February 1943, the British cargo steamer Ascot arrived in Colombo on her maiden voyage, the temporary solution to the Indian food shortage had become an established routine, with a steady stream of ships bringing grain, in bulk, from Australia. Consequently, instead of returning to the UK after the discharge of her outward cargo, the Ascot found herself joining the "food train" between Calcutta and Fremantle, an assignment which was to last for the next twelve months. For her crew, the interlude was not an unpleasant one, the heat, filth and frustration of India being offset by the long, relaxing ocean passages and the attractions of that other world to the south, where life was orderly, clean and hospitable.

The 7005-ton Ascot came out of a Dundee shipyard on a grey, rainswept day in November 1942. To her owners, the world-wide traders Watts, Watts & Company of London, who had a reputation for building ships a cut above the ordinary tramp, she may have seemed somewhat utilitarian, but there was no room for frills in this third year of total war. At 419 ft long and 57 ft in the beam, she was a deep-gutted, no nonsense cargo carrier, and nothing more. On her trials her coal-burning engines achieved a maximum speed of 10 knots, probably for the first and last time in her sea-going career. In reality, her average speed would never be in excess of 9 knots – and that only in fair weather.

Captain James Fawcett Travis, appointed to command the Ascot, harboured no grand illusions about his new ship, but was confident that, being Dundee-built, she was stout and reliable. When he joined the ship, 35-year-old Jack Travis, a native of Hull, now settled in Oban, brought with him a crew of 45. His senior men, Chief Officer Claude Blackett and Chief Engineer William Ewing, hailed from

North Shields and Aberdeen respectively, 68-year-old Ewing having postponed his retirement for the duration of the war. From Travis's native Hull, came Second Officer William Crowther, Third Officer Charles Hatton, First Radio Officer J. Hamilton and Second Radio Officer Dennis Deveney. The Ascot's deck and catering ratings were drawn mainly from Dundee, while her firemen were a gang of hard-working West Indians. At the bottom of the shipboard ladder were two 18-year-old apprentices, Harry Fortune of Hartlepool and Anthony Taylor of Chippenham. By and large then, the Ascot was a ship of the north, but with many diverse accents to be heard in her alleyways. More importantly, she was manned by men who knew the business of the sea.

One of the last jobs to be done on the Ascot, in the fitting-out basin was the mounting of her armament, with which, it was hoped, she would be able to deter her enemies on the high seas. In a very short time she was equipped with a 4-inch anti-submarine gun, four 20mm Oerlikons, two twin Hotchkiss machine-guns and a multiple rocket launcher, known as a "pillar box." The maintenance and manning of these guns would be in the capable hands of the last crew members to join, a team of ten DEMS gunners, led by Sergeant W. Hughson, Royal Marines, a tough Shetland islander.

After loading her first cargo in Birkenhead, the Ascot sailed in mid-January 1943, arriving in Colombo at the end of February. During the course of the next twelve months, the make-up of her crew underwent a considerable change, becoming even more cosmopolitan. On the initial leg of the voyage, her boatswain, chief steward and two ABs took sick and were landed into hospital in the Red Sea. Later, the sensuous charms of Australia took their usual toll, no fewer than six Scots ratings disappearing into the outback, never to return again. Replacements included Chief Steward J. Gottschalk of London, Maltese boatswain C. Aquis, Australian second cook Frank Jordan,

Greek able seaman P. Karaopoulos and Dutch seaman M. van Bekhoven. But, although her strong North British identity was somewhat diluted by the newcomers, under Jack Travis the Ascot remained a tight ship in all respects.

Crew changes apart, the Ascot's first year at sea was relatively uneventful, her energies devoted almost exclusively to feeding starving India. When she left Colombo, on 19 February 1944, bound for Fremantle via Diego Suarez, she was loaded with 9000 tons of pig iron, paraffin wax, gunnies, linseed oil, coconuts and fibre; a fair exchange for the grain she would return with. The passage to Madagascar was expected to take at least twelve days, for after a year tramping in these warm, fecund waters the steamer's bottom was encrusted with barnacles and trailing long streamers of weed. Even at the hands of the experienced Bill Ewing, her coal-burning engines would be unlikely to deliver more than 7 knots under a full head of steam. It was certainly not to Jack Travis's liking, to have to trail his coat across the Indian Ocean at the speed of a sluggish bicycle, but he had no alternative. It was, therefore, of some consolation to him that, up until the time of sailing from Colombo, there had been no reports of enemy submarines operating in the area through which he was about to steam.

Captain Jack Travis (centre) at launching of the Ascot Dundee, 1942

Three days out from Colombo the Ascot passed through the One-and-a-Half Degree Channel, a gap in the thousand-plus island archi-pelago of the Maldives, and then altered course for the northern tip of Madagascar. The weather continued fine and clear, the sea calm and the wind in the north-east and light. The Indian Ocean at its best. On the morning of the 28th, roughly halfway between the Seychelles and Diego Garcia, Travis received a wireless message from the Admiralty ordering him to divert further to the west and to cease zig-zagging at midnight. Travis thought the two orders appeared contradictory, the first seeming to indicate danger, while the second could be construed as a sign that all danger was past. But, being bound to radio silence, he was unable to clarify the message with Colombo and, accordingly, as from midnight that night, the Ascot ceased to zig-zag.

Noon on the 29th, saw the usual midday activity on the bridge of the Ascot. Sun sights had been taken and both Second Officer William Crowther and Third Officer Charles Hatton were at work with almanacs and log tables. Captain Travis, as befitted his rank, paced the wheelhouse awaiting the results of the calculations. It was a particularly fine day, with clear blue skies, an even bluer sea and the wind blowing from astern with just enough force to ease the Ascot on her way. Moving out into the port wing of the bridge, Travis stood in the shade of the canvas awning and idly scanned the horizon ahead. The line between sea and sky was blurring slightly in the heat of the sun, but was unencumbered by ships or land, as it had been for the past ten days. The noon sights were expected to confirm that the Ascot was 5 degrees south of the Equator and some 450 miles due east of the Seychelles. Five more days steaming should see the mountains of Madagascar in sight. The island, recently wrested from the Vichy French in a brilliant operation involving British and South African troops, was something of an unknown quantity to Travis. He speculated on what their reception would be when they reached Diego Suarez.

Jack Travis's contemplation of the future would have been less pleasant if he had known his ship was being observed by hostile eyes, for close on the Ascot's starboard bow, and out of Travis's line of sight, a periscope had just broken the surface. Since disposing of the Sutlej and most of her crew on the evening of the 26th, I-37 had moved 480 miles to the north-west and was lying in wait for her next victim. As Lieutenant-Commander Nakagawa studied the deep-laden Ascot through his periscope he could not suppress a grunt of satisfaction. This was another fat one to add to his bag – and steaming so slow he could hardly miss.

Gunner G. Kiel of the Maritime Regiment, on watch on the after gun platform, was the only man to see Nakagawa's torpedo speeding towards the Ascot. He dived for the telephone to warn the bridge, but was too late. The torpedo struck the ship in the fore part of her engine-room on the starboard side. There was a dull explosion and the Ascot reeled heavily to port. A huge column of water, debris and coal dust shot skywards and fell back, deluging the gun platform, where Kiel and his watchmate were valiantly attempting to ready the 4-inch for action. Both men were knocked off their feet by the force of the water and the Ascot's only means of striking back, was rendered impotent.

The engine-room was ripped open by the 21-inch Japanese torpedo, the sea flooded in, dousing the fires in the Ascot's boilers and cutting off the steam to her main engine. Twenty-one-year-old, Third Engineer G. Gibson and the three West Indians in his watch, died before they could make a move to escape to the deck. The crippled ship slowly righted herself and began to settle bodily.

Second Radio Officer Dennis Deveney, on watch in the wireless room, quickly acquainted himself with the situation on the bridge, switched on his transmitter and began to tap out the letters SSS, the submarine attack distress signal. His efforts were in vain, for, predictably, both main and emergency aerials had been brought down by the explosion. The Ascot was on her own.

Eighteen-year-old Apprentice Harry Fortune was in his cabin, hands and face scrubbed, and hungrily awaiting the lunch bell when the torpedo struck. Hunger was immediately replaced by the need to survive and Fortune headed for boat deck at a run.

No signal had yet been given to abandon ship, but when Fortune reached the boat deck he found Captain Travis and Chief Officer Blackett supervising the launching of the lifeboats amidst a certain amount of chaos. Both starboard lifeboats had been reduced to matchwood by the explosion and what should have been a reasonably straightforward operation – given the ship was still upright – seemed to be going wrong at every turn. The first boat to be lowered ran away, crashed to the water, and drifted off, apparently severely damaged. The remaining boat also narrowly escaped disaster, fouling its own painter as it was being lowered and almost capsizing. Luckily, this boat was cleared before serious harm was done and 34 men, Harry Fortune among them, boarded and pushed off from the sinking ship's side. Others took to the water and clambered onto the only life raft to be launched. Once clear of the ship, the damaged lifeboat was retrieved and Travis distributed his men more equally between the boats and the raft. Blackett took charge of the damaged boat and the three craft hurriedly pulled away from the ship, which they feared might go down at any moment.

They had not rowed far when, with a rush of compressed air, I-37 came to the surface 2000 yards off the Ascot's starboard quarter. Fortune, who was one of those assigned to the raft, watched as the grey-painted submarine, her casings streaked with rust, circled the ship once, then opened fire on it with her deck gun. The shelling went on for some fifteen minutes, but the Japanese aim was not good, and they scored no hits.

As the survivors lay back on their oars waiting for the inevitable destruction of their ship, they heard the submarine's motors roar into life again, and with black smoke pouring from her twin exhausts, I-37 slewed around and headed towards them. This was the moment they had been dreading. Harry Fortune, his keen young mind working overtime, studied the submarine carefully as she drew near. Her deck gun, which appeared to be a 6-inch, was manned by five men dressed in khaki shirts, slacks and soft peaked caps. An Oerlikon-type anti-aircraft gun protruded from a blister at the side of her conning tower and a light machine gun, similar to a Bren, was mounted on the tower. She carried no national markings, but Fortune knew she must be Japanese.

He gave an involuntary shiver. Tales of the bestiality of these people were rife.

The submarine stopped with Blackett's boat and the raft on her port side and Travis's boat to starboard. The raft was only a matter of yards from the casings of the sub and Fortune had a clear view of the men on board. They were undoubtedly Japanese. One of their number, who appeared to be in command, hailed the boats, in English, calling on the captain, chief officer and wireless operator to identify themselves. Fortune and his companions were well briefed on this routine and immediately answered that all three men were dead. While this exchange was going on, Fortune took the opportunity to examine the submarine's crew. At least fifteen were on deck, four in the conning tower and the rest on the forward casing. Among the latter was one who stood out like a sore thumb. He wore the same untidy khakis as the rest, but he was much taller and wore a European-style peaked cap with a gold badge. He looked like, and most probably was, a German. An advisor or observer, perhaps?

Having extracted no useful information from the survivors on his port side, Lieutenant-Commander Nakagawa now turned his attention to the boat lying to starboard of I-37. A burst of machine-gun fire was directed across the bows of the boat – obviously as a warning – and the demands were repeated. Jack Travis, knowing he could no longer hide behind his men, stood up and acknowledged that he was the master of the ship. He was instructed to bring the boat alongside the sub and was then taken aboard and ordered to point out his chief officer. This Travis did and Blackett was brought on board, but apparently only to confirm Travis's identity, for having done so, the chief officer was allowed to return to the boat.

And that, it seemed, was that. The Japanese appeared to be following the German U-boat practice of taking the master of the ship out of circulation, leaving any other survivors to fend for themselves, until, in full view of the horrified watchers in the boats, Nakagawa showed his true colours. With a cry of "English swine!" he slashed the palms of Travis's hands with his sword and pushed him overboard.

Despite his injuries, Travis managed to swim to the nearest lifeboat and was hauled aboard. Meanwhile, Harry Fortune and his fellow survivors on the raft had taken the opportunity to paddle surreptitiously away from the submarine. It was just as well they had, for Nakagawa now launched into a frenzy of wanton murder that was to last for two ghastly hours.

The Japanese commander began by ramming the two lifeboats, spilling the survivors into the sea, and then opened fire on them with a machine-gun sited on the conning tower. It was systematic murder; the brutal killing of innocent, helpless men who had nowhere to hide. The submarine cruised relentlessly up and down between the boats and the men in the water, firing continuously. Blackett's boat, already partially waterlogged, turned over and sank. The silence of the Indian Ocean was shattered by the screams of the dying, its once untroubled surface gradually turning from blue to blood red.

Fortune was quick to see the machine-gun being brought into action and called to the men on the raft to dive overboard. Some did, others stayed where they were and died. The apprentice and six others who had followed him over the side survived only by keeping the bullet-riddled raft between themselves and the Japanese.

At last Nakagawa, his blood lust temporarily sated, turned his attention back to the Ascot, which, although sagging low in the water, was still very much afloat. While he was thus occupied, those survivors who were left alive reboarded the remaining lifeboat and raft. Many were wounded, all were in a state of shock. As he hoisted himself back onto the bloodstained raft, Fortune was relieved to see that Captain Travis was alive, and had taken charge of the boat. A tow rope was passed to the raft and, with Travis at the helm, the boat set off to clear the area as quickly as possible. They had not progressed far when the rope broke and the raft was left drifting, at this point Nakagawa, having pumped 30 shells into the Ascot and set her ablaze, decided to return to finish off his grisly work.

Fortune was first to realise the submarine was intent on ramming the raft first, and, with a shout of warning to the others, he again threw himself into the sea. He was not a moment too soon, the bullets scythed into the water around him as he dived.

Two men were left on the raft, both DEMS gunners. Able Seaman Richardson, a bullet in his thigh from the initial attack, was delirious, and Gunner T. Walker had stayed with him. Showing superb courage, Walker shielded Richardson with his body, and at the same time kept those in the water informed of the sub's movements. Sadly, Walker's efforts to save Richardson failed. A swathe of bullets sweeping across the raft caught the Royal Navy man in the chest and he died instantly. Walker, wounded in the leg and thigh, feigned death.

Nakagawa spent a further two hours on his grim task of eliminating the remaining Ascot survivors, killing and maiming with apparent relish. When, at 20.00 that night, I-37 motored away, she took the abandoned and bullet-riddled lifeboat with her, leaving anyone still alive to the mercy of the sharks.

But the Japanese butcher had not been thorough enough. The raft still remained afloat and, as soon as the sound of the submarine's throbbing exhausts died away, there were signs of life in the bloody waters. Seven men dragged themselves aboard the raft. Harry Fortune and his fellow apprentice Anthony Taylor were first to board; they were followed by Frank Jordan, the Ascot's second cook, Able Seaman P. Karaopoulos and Able Seaman M. van Bekhoven. Then came the wounded, but uncomplaining, Gunner Walker, helped aboard by Gunner Kiel, the first man to sight the enemy's torpedo eight long hours before. Harry Fortune, still a mere boy, but the senior in rank, took charge, and once the fresh blood had been washed from the raft, settled his men down to wait out the night. An hour and a half later they watched the glow from the Ascot's fires quenched as she slipped beneath the sea.

The night was long but darkness clothed the carnage, until it was revealed at dawn, on the first day of March. The sea surrounding the raft was littered with the pathetic remains of the Ascot and the lifeless bodies of most of her crew. It soon became obvious to the seven men, occupying the blood stained and broken raft, they were all that remained of the 56 men who had sailed out of Colombo eleven days earlier.

There was no time for anger or grief. As the sun came up Fortune sighted an object on the horizon that looked suspiciously like the conning tower of a submarine. The Japanese had come back to finish their work. As the raft was now surrounded by marauding barracudas there could be no question of taking to the water again. Fate must be allowed to have its way.

The gods were with Harry Fortune and his men on that St David's Day – despite the fact there was not a Welshman amongst them. The approaching "submarine" turned out to be nothing more lethal than the Ascot's only remaining lifeboat, riddled by bullets and floating on its buoyancy tanks. The raft's sail was hoisted and the paddles came out, but another day passed before they were able to come alongside the boat. Inside they found Sergeant Hughson with a bullet wound in his head but still very much alive. Hughson told of how he had been hit before he could jump overboard and had feigned death when the Japanese towed the boat away. About two miles from the Ascot, the boat was cast off and then rammed again. Next day, although the boat was waterlogged and its stern smashed, Hughson had hoisted the jib sail before he collapsed from loss of blood.

Fortune decided the damaged boat would be of little use to them, and transferred the injured Royal Marine sergeant, and the provisons from the boat's tanks into the raft. The raft's fresh water tank was intact and Fortune calculated that, with careful rationing, they would be able to survive for at least three weeks. The wind was in the north-east and he had no choice but to run before it, in the general direction of Madagascar, some 900 miles to the south-west.

As luck would have it, the awesome voyage did not come to pass. At 11.00 that morning a ship was sighted, which proved to be the Dutch motor vessel Straat Soenda. Harry Fortune and his companions were picked up and landed at Aden six days later, a brave little band of eight, all that was left to tell the tale of the blood-bath of 29 February.

When Nakagawa took I-37 back to her base in Penang, he left behind him three separate groups of survivors, 39 men of the British Chivalry crowded into one leaking lifeboat, 29 men of the Sutlej in a lifeboat and two rafts, and the 8 survivors from the Ascot on a damaged raft. The odds against any of these surviving living for more than a few days had been great and their abandonment, alone, was a heinous crime. As to the 118 men of these three ships, who died at Nakagawa's hands, most of them murdered in cold blood, this was brutality in the extreme, marking the Japanese submarine commander as one of the most notorious butchers ever to sail the high seas.

I-37's reign of terror came to an end with the sinking of the Ascot. She claimed no more victims and, nine months later, on 12 November, she was sunk, with all hands, off the Pacific island of Yap by the US destroyer Nicholas. Nakagawa was not in command at the time.

NINE

It could be said that Japan's "Pearl Harbor" came on 17 February 1944, when a large force of US carrier-borne aircraft bombed Truk Atoll, the Imperial Fleet's safe anchorage in the Pacific. The attack began under the cover of a storm and lasted for almost 48 hours. With characteristic thoroughness, American planes saturated the atoll with bombs, sinking two light cruisers, four destroyers, three armed merchant cruisers, two submarine tenders and twenty-four merchant ships, a total of 200,000 tons of shipping. In addition, more than 200 Japanese planes were destroyed and the island's oil tanks set ablaze when US battleships joined in the assault.

Truk was yet another devastating blow to the Japanese. They saw their ill-gotten power in the Pacific waning, while the Americans grew ever stronger and pushed relentlessly northwards. It seemed certain the Marianas would be next to fall, then the Philippines, until, as surely as day follows night, the homeland itself came under threat. For a people who in two short years had come so near to dominating much of Asia and Oceania, this was an appalling prospect to face.

But at sea all was not lost. Through the foresight of Admiral Koga, who replaced Yamamoto, the bulk of the Japanese fleet had been withdrawn from Truk a week before the attack to bases further west, including Singapore and Penang. Smarting under their failure to contain the Americans in the Pacific, the Japanese admirals then turned to the Indian Ocean, where Admiral Somerville's British forces were still very thinly spread.

On 26 February, the 16th Squadron of the Japanese South-West Area Fleet, under the command of Vice-Admiral Naomasa Sakonju, slipped out of Penang and steamed south-east through the Malacca Straits. The plan was to enter the Indian Ocean via the Sunda Strait and embark on a vigorous campaign against Allied merchant shipping. The squadron consisted of the heavy cruisers Aoba, Chikuma and Tone, all veterans of Pearl Harbor, the Java Sea and Midway. These 12,000-ton ships had a top speed of 35 knots and were armed with 8-inch guns. Sakonju's orders from Penang were to seek out and, where possible, capture Allied ships. Should it become necessary to sink a ship, prisoners were to be taken, but "only the minimum needed for interrogation." Ominously, no orders were given, in relation to any other survivors. One man – perhaps the only Japanese officer – not entirely happy with this particular edict was Captain Haruo Mayazumi, commander of the Tone. Mayazumi was a rare breed of Japanese, he was a Christian, with religious beliefs worlds apart from the code of Bushido. In the weeks to come, a conflict of loyalties was to play havoc with Mayazumi's well-ordered life.

The three ships, with Admiral Sakonju flying his flag in Aoba, rounded the south-eastern tip of Sumatra on the 28th and passed through the Sunda Strait into the Indian Ocean. There they fanned out and began patrolling to the south of the Cocos Islands, where they hoped to fall in with Allied shipping sailing between Australia and the Indian sub-continent.

Twenty-four hours after the Japanese cruisers cleared the Sunda Strait, the British passenger/cargo vessel Behar sailed from Melbourne in a blaze of publicity she could have done without. The 7840-ton Behar, owned by the Hain Steamship Company, was on her maiden voyage and it had not escaped the notice of the Australian Press that she was more than a cut above the usual, rather basic, merchantman being turned out by British shipyards at the time. The Melbourne papers, rather unwisely, gave her a write-up that must have seemed like manna from heaven to Japanese Intelligence.

Completed at Barclay Curle's yard on the Clyde at the end of May 1943, the Behar was a replacement for an earlier ship of that name sunk by a mine in Milford Haven in November 1940. She was a twin-screw motor ship, powered by Doxford engines which gave her a service speed of 16œ knots, and she carried the latest in navigational gear. Her twelve passenger cabins were of a standard comparable with the best in the big liners of pre-war days, and her officers' accommodation had a matching air of luxury, hardly to be expected in the nineteen forties. Her owners, a subsidiary of the top-ranking P & O Company, were patently casting their eyes to the future when, with the war relegated to the history books, the passenger trade would come back into its own. As to the depressing necessities of war, the Behar was equally well served, being one of the few British merchant ships to carry both Asidic and depth charges. Her deck armament was also formidable, consisting of one 4-inch and one 3-inch dual purpose guns, a multiple rocket launcher, 20-mm Oerlikons and .5-inch Browning machine-guns.

The Behar carried a total crew of 102, made up of 18 British officers, 17 DEMS gunners and asidic operators, and 67 Indian ratings. Her master, 51-year-old Captain Maurice Symonds, was West Country born but living in Glasgow, while 58-year-old James Weir was the archetypal Glaswegian chief engineer to be found in all good sea fiction. Under him, Weir had a team of seven Scots engineers, all of whom had kept watch over the ship while she was fitting out on the Clyde. Her engines were in good hands. The senior man on the navigation side was Chief Officer William Phillips, 38, of Cardiff, and sharing the bridge watches with him were Second Officer Gordon Rowlandson, Third Officer James Anderson, Fourth Officer John Robertson, and apprentices Denys Matthews and Alan Moore. Three wireless operators, First Radio Officer Arthur Walker, Second Radio Officer James Smyth, and Third Radio Officer Henry Cummings, another Glaswegian, kept round-the-clock watches in the radio room. The DEMS personnel, drawn from the Royal Navy and the Maritime Regiment, were led by Petty Officer W.L. Griffiths. The Behar was, without doubt, a well-built, well-equipped, well-manned ship, and all those who sailed in her, were proud to do so.

Having loaded her first cargo in Liverpool in the late summer of 1943, the Behar took up her ill-fated predecessor's role, trading between the United Kingdom and Australasia, calling at ports in South Africa and India on route. She left Melbourne on 19 February 1944 to return to the UK, carrying a part-cargo of 796 tons of zinc. She was to call at Bombay and other Indian coast ports to complete her homeward loading.

Occupying the Behar's comfortable passenger cabins when she left Melbourne were Duncan MacGregor, a retired Australian bank manager on his way to Kenya via Bombay, Captain P.J. Green of the Indo China Steam Navigation Company, three Royal New Zealand Navy officers, an RAF flight sergeant, Dr Lai Young Li, a Chinese physician, and two wives of dockyard officials stationed in Calcutta. The passage to Bombay, a distance of 5558 miles, was expected to take just under 15 days, fine weather, it was predicted, prevailing all the way.

On the run across the Great Australian Bight, problems were experienced with the Behar's minesweeping paravanes, resulting in her being delayed for some twelve hours. Captain Symonds, already troubled by the press coverage his ship had received in Melbourne, was not pleased. He could have had no idea how disastrous this delay would prove for his ship and himself.

Cape Leeuwin was passed on the night of 4 March and course was set for India. Over the next four days, the ship pushed north-westwards, eating up the miles at a steady 16 knots. The weather, as anticipated, proved excellent, giving the passengers the opportunity of taking to their deck chairs, while the Behar's crew, on watch and off, enjoyed the peace of an empty, undisturbed ocean. The news bulletins from London, posted each day by the radio officers, glowed with justified optimism. Allied troops were ashore in Italy and marching northwards, despite determined German opposition, while in Russia the siege of Leningrad had been lifted and Hitler's panzers, faced with heavy Russian counterattacks, were falling back in disarray. There was even guarded talk of the Second Front, a return across the Channel by Allied troops. But, for those in the Behar, the most encouraging news of all came from Burma, where the incredible Japanese war machine was at last weakening. A Japanese offensive against the British 14th Army in the Arakan had been smashed by men under the command of Lieutenant-General Slim. This, the first British land victory against the Japanese, had seen the enemy fleeing into the jungle, leaving behind more than 5000 dead. The tide was turning.

On reaching a position 500 miles south of the Cocos Islands on 1 March, Admiral Sakonju's heavy cruisers began to sweep industriously back and forth across the trade route between India and Australia. The three ships, Aoba, Chikuma and Tone, steamed in line abreast and just out of sight of each other, covering a broad swathe of the Indian Ocean some 60 miles wide. It was monotonous, demoralising work, for day after day the horizon remained stubbornly empty. When dawn came on the 9th, the cruisers were nearing the westernmost point of yet another fruitless sweep and Sakonju had begun to give thought to casting his net elsewhere. The sun came up, and with it came a sea haze, reducing the visibility to less than two miles. This helped to make up the Admiral's mind; when the end of the sweep was reached he would take his ships to the north. Then, at about 09.00, shortly before the cruisers were to alter course, a keen-eyed lookout at the masthead of the Tone sighted smoke on the horizon. Captain Mayazumi increased speed and moved in to investigate.

Had it not been for the 12-hour delay suffered in the Australian Bight, the Behar would have been 200 miles further to the north on the morning of the 9th, and well out of reach of the searching Japanese cruisers. It was just pure bad luck that the Tone stumbled upon her.

Twenty-three-year-old Third Officer James Anderson had the watch on the bridge of the Behar when, at a few minutes before 10.00, the 12,000-ton Tone, her huge gun turrets already trained, emerged from the mist on the starboard beam. Initially Anderson thought that they had crossed paths with the Royal Navy, but when he examined the approaching warship through his binoculars, something about the rake of her funnel aroused his suspicions. He called Captain Symonds to the bridge.

Symonds arrived in time to see the Tone's signal lamp flash a terse order for the Behar to heave-to. It was immediately apparent to him the challenger was an enemy warship and he lost no time in instructing the wireless room to send out a distress prefixed by the code RRR (I am being attacked by a surface raider). Third Radio Officer Henry Cumming, on watch at the time, switched on his transmitter and began sending. This proved to be a fatal mistake. The Japanese ship's operators were on the alert, and no sooner had Cumming's first burst of morse gone out over the air, than the cruiser hoisted her colours and opened fire.

The first salvo of 8-inch shells fell a mere 30 yards short of the Behar, ricochetted off the water, and then burst on the British ship's foredeck with devastating effect. Chief Officer William Phillips was in his cabin below the bridge pressing a spare pair of trousers with a hot iron. The exploding shells put an abrupt end to this rare moment of domesticity. Phillips calmly switched off the iron and made his way to the bridge to join Symonds and Anderson.

From then on chaos reigned, the Tone, firing at point blank range, poured shell after shell into the Behar, blasting great holes in her hull below the waterline and turning her decks into a burning shambles. Petty Officer Griffiths and his men made a valiant attempt to man their guns, but such was the ferocity of the Japanese cruiser's attack they were unable to fire a single shot before the cry went up to abandon ship. The Behar was sinking.

With the ship still under heavy bombardment, it was a tribute to the tight discipline and courage of her crew that the Behar's four lifeboats were launched successfully. It had already been established nine persons were missing, including the two women passengers, and as soon as the boats were in the water Symonds and Phillips, who remained on board, began a careful search of the burning ship. Working from forward to aft, the two men groped their way through the smoke and flames, crouching low to avoid the shrapnel flying over their heads. Before long they came across the bodies of two DEMS gunners and an Indian seaman, cut down by the shelling, which did not auger well for the others. However, Chief Engineer James Weir appeared out of the smoke unharmed, having gone below to ensure the engines were stopped and the engine-room evacuated. Inside the passenger accommodation the two women and an Indian steward were discovered, badly frightened, but uninjured. Petty Officer Griffiths was also found alive. He had stayed behind to dispose of secret Navy documents before abandoning ship.

By this time the lifeboats had pulled away from the ship and the six survivors were forced to go over the rail into the water, for the Behar was settling fast. Griffiths was picked up by one of the boats almost at once, but the others became lost in the mist and it was some time before they were found. Clinging to pieces of wreckage, Symonds and Phillips were mute witnesses to the dying throes of the ship they had been so proud to serve in. The Behar, not yet a year old, went down with dignity twenty minutes after the first Japanese shells had found her.

The four lifeboats now came together, and after a careful head-count, it was found that out of the 111 on board the Behar, only three men were missing, and their bodies had been seen by Symonds and Phillips. Considering the savage and unprovoked bombardment the ship had suffered, the casualty list was remarkably low. Having established this, Captain Symonds was faced with the problem of saving the lives of the 108 souls crowded into the four boats under his command. The nearest land, not under occupation by the Japanese, Australia, lay 1200 miles to the east, a long and hazardous voyage to undertake. Symonds was discussing a plan of action with Phillips when the Tone once more appeared out of the mist.

They feared the Japanese cruiser was about to ram the boats, but her engines were seen to go astern and she hove-to several hundred yards off. Then a loud hailer was switched on and a tinny voice ordered the boats alongside. The Behar's survivors were reluctant to comply, but men armed with rifles and machine-guns appeared at the cruiser's rails, leaving no sensible alternative. When the boats touched, boarding ladders were thrown over the side and Chief Officer Phillips, Captain Green, and Petty Officer Griffiths were the first men up.

A line of grim-faced Japanese sailors, with levelled rifles, greeted the three men as they arrived on the deck of the cruiser – a reception committee William Phillips viewed with a sinking feeling in his stomach.

His fears were well founded, for he was seized by rough hands and relieved of most of his clothing, before being trussed up with his hands behind his back and a rope looped around his neck. The others, including the women, received the same treatment as they climbed the rail. Phillips protested vehemently, pointing out this was a flagrant breach of the Geneva Convention. For his troubles he received a severe beating with a baseball bat. On his knees and bleeding, he continued to protest, and when a Japanese officer arrived, the women were released.

For some hours the bound survivors were made to sit on the deck in the hot sun like so many sacrificial lambs, then they were herded below decks and bundled into a small, unlit storeroom. Here their Japanese guards set about them with bamboo batons. The beatings were brutal, systematic and totally unwarranted. Phillips, who through his protests was a primary target for the batons, assumed this was a softening up process, and a very effective one at that. Later in the day, when they were close to suffocation in the cramped space, the survivors' bonds were untied and they were moved to a larger compartment. Their new prison, although allowing more movement, was also badly lit and poorly ventilated. The heat generated by more than a hundred breathing, sweating bodies soon turned it into a heaving sauna.

There followed six days of incarceration in this sweat-box, during which time the prisoners received little food or water. Hunger and thirst combined with the claustrophobic nature of their prison to reduce morale to rock bottom. Twice a day, and once during each night, they were allowed on deck in small groups for short periods of exercise. Crude latrines rigged over the ship's side and a small bowl of fresh water each for washing were the only toilet facilities provided. Common criminals in any reasonable jail would have received, better treatment.

During his first visit to the deck, at night, Phillips studied the stars closely and established the cruiser was heading in a north-easterly direction, probably towards the Sunda Strait. This gave rise to the conclusion that the ultimate destination was Japan, and led to many long hours of speculation below decks, on what might happen to them on arrival. Sitting out the rest of the war in a Japanese prisoner of war camp was not a prospect any of the survivors looked forward to, and they did not envisage anything worse. Then, on the night of the 14th, the stars told Phillips the ship had changed course to due east. He assumed they were through the Sunda Strait, and definitely not heading for Japan.

Early next morning, for the first time in six days, the beat of the cruiser's engines slowed, and then stopped. In the semi-darkness of the prison below decks the Behar's survivors waited expectantly. They were not surprised when the ship began to vibrate as her engines went astern. The faint rattle of an anchor chain confirmed that the Tone had come to an anchorage. Rough calculations based on William Phillips's night-time observations made it highly likely they were somewhere off the north coast of Java. Some hours later, when they were finally brought up on deck into the brilliant sunshine, they saw they were in a sheltered bay with two other heavy cruisers anchored nearby. These, they were to learn later, were Admiral Sakonju's flagship, Aoba, and the third member of the 16th Squadron, the Chikuma. The anchorage was off Tandjong Priok, the port for Java's capital city, Batavia, and only 50 miles east of the Sunda Strait.

The Behar survivors, were not aware, as they sat on deck drinking in the fresh air and sunlight, that a vigorous argument over their ultimate fate had been raging for some days. When he sank the Behar on the 9th, the Tone's commander, Captain Mayazumi, immediately signalled Vice-Admiral Sakonju, in the Aoba, telling him of his success. Instead of the expected congratulations, Mayazumi received a sharp rebuke. Sakonju pointed out that the squadron had explicit orders to, whenever possible, capture Allied ships, not to sink them, and he demanded to know why Mayazumi had not followed this course with the Behar. In retrospect, there seems no good reason why Mayazumi did not put a prize crew on the British ship, for she offered no opposition. Her cargo of zinc would have been of great value to the Japanese war effort, and the fast, brand new ship, would have been a welcome addition to its dwindling merchant fleet. Mayazumi's defence, that he was too far away from base to have successfully brought the Behar in under her own steam was, to say the least, feeble. He had, however, scored the only success of the patrol, a fact Sakonju choose to ignore, as he berated his junior.

If Sakonju was annoyed at the unnecessary sinking of the Behar, then he was furious when he discovered the Tone had 108 prisoners on board. He reminded Mayazumi that his orders also specified quite clearly, only the minimum number of prisoners required for interrogation were to be taken. Having apologised profusely for his negligence, the unfortunate Mayazumi asked what he was to do with the surplus prisoners. He was curtly told by Sakonju to "dispose of them." There could be no mistaking Sakonju's meaning. This was an order to execute.

For most officers of the Japanese Imperial Navy, the situation would have posed no problem, their duty clearly being to obey implicity the orders of a superior without questioning the morality of these orders. Mayazumi, on the other hand, was faced with a massive conflict of interests; his Christian faith would not allow him to condone the murder of innocents – for that is what it would be. He discussed the matter with his second-in-command, Commander Mii, who for reasons not known, also disagreed with Sakonju's edict. Captain Mayazumi then sent a signal to the Aoba pleading that he be allowed to land all his prisoners at Tandjong Priok. The reply came back,

"Dispose of prisoners immediately!" But when the Tone reached the anchorage on the 15th, all her prisoners were still alive. Mayazumi's Christian faith, inherited from St Francis Xavier, who planted the seeds in Kagoshima nearly 400 years earlier, had proved to be the dominant side of the captain's character.

As soon as his ship was safely anchored at Tandjong Priok, Mayazumi called for his launch, crossed to the Aoba and courageously confronted the Admiral. He went on his knees before Sakonju and begged that the innocents of the Behar be allowed to live. Naomasa Sakonju was unmoved, and in the face of his wrath Mayazumi's religious faith faltered and was swamped by his ingrained Japanese obedience to the will of a superior. He returned to the Tone, a very subdued man, to inform Mii that, as soon as the cruiser sailed from Tandjong Priok, the execution must be carried out. It only remained to decide who was to live and who was to die.

The separating of the sacrificial sheep from the fold, took place on the deck of the Tone that same morning. Captain Symonds, Chief Officer Phillips, Chief Engineer Weir, Second Engineer McGinnes, First Radio Officer Walker, Petty Officer Griffiths, the two Asdic ratings and twenty-one English speaking Indian ratings were taken to one side. They were then transferred to the Aoba along with seven of the nine passengers, including Captain Green, Dr Lai Young Li and the two women. As the party contained the most senior of the Behar's personnel, it appeared to those left behind the Japanese must have some form of intensive interrogation in mind and, ironically, they feared for the safety of Symonds and the others. They had no inkling of the gross obscenity about to befall them.

A few hours later, the Tone weighed anchor and put to sea, taking with her, on their last voyage the 72 Behar survivors who were surplus to Vice-Admiral Sakonju's requirements. That evening Captain Mayazumi instructed Commander Mii to execute the prisoners. Mii, who turned out to be the more humane and stronger willed of the two men, refused to be associated with the deed. Mayazumi, himself in mental torment, was forced to issue a direct order for the execution to the next man in the chain of command, Lieutenant Ishihara. Late that night, Ishihara, in company with Lieutenant Tani, Sub-Lieutenant Tanaka, Sub-Lieutenant Otsuka and several other officers, lined the prisoners up on deck. At the subsequent war crimes trial it was revealed that all 72 were butchered like animals in a slaughterhouse, each man being felled with a blow to the stomach before being beheaded. The scuppers of the Japanese cruiser ran red with the blood of those innocent souls on that tranquil night in the Java Sea. Never, in the recent annals of maritime history, has such a barbarous deed been recorded.

Captain Symonds and his party, much to their surprise, were not questioned aboard the Aoba, but were put ashore in Tandjong Priok. The Europeans were imprisoned in a small room of a building that had once been the local office of the Royal Interoccan Lines, where they spent an uncomfortable night, ignorant of the terrible fate of the other survivors. Next day, they were joined by the Indian ratings. If the makeshift prison had been crowded before, with another 21 people packed in, it was unbearable. Their complaints to the guards went unheeded, but much to their relief, two days later, on 18 March, they were moved to a prisoner of war camp outside Batavia. On arrival at the camp, Phillips, who had never let up in his protests against their inhuman treatment, was immediately put into solitary confinement. Bound hand and foot, with a bamboo lashed across his throat to prevent sleep, he was thrown into a tiny wooden shed, on the outskirts of the camp, no larger than a dog kennel. Through a small knothole he watched the change from light to darkness and back again as the days crawled by and his physical agony increased. But William Phillips was a resilient man and retained his sanity by forcing his brain to carry out

long and intricate feats of mental arithmetic, at the same time study-
ing the progress of a young plant growing within range of his tiny win-
dow on the world.

The Japanese in Batavia showed a modicum of compassion for the
two women prisoners by sending them to a separate women's camp.
The men were kept together, but in isolation from the rest of the
camp, and over the months that followed, suffered severe privation,
beatings and continuous interrogation by their guards. Eventually,
when it was finally accepted nothing of value could be wrung from the
Behar's men, they were split up, Captain Symonds, Captain Green
and First Radio Officer Walker being sent to Japan to work in the
mines. The remainder were moved into the main body of the camp,
where they were joined by William Phillips, whose incarceration had
also been of no material help to Japanese Intelligence.

The camp, deep in the rain forests of Java, held British, Australian,
American and Dutch servicemen and civilians. The Japanese provided
only a starvation diet and took particular pleasure in humiliating the
disgraced and despised whites by forcing them to work from dawn to
dusk, clearing the ground around the camp of vegetation, using only
their bare hands as tools. Many went mad and were forced into the
surrounding jungle, there to starve or be devoured by wild animals.
The only means of escape was through death.

For fifteen long months Phillips and his fellow prisoners endured
this hell on earth, and all the time without the faintest hope of deliverance. In July 1945, when it became obvious, even to the Japanese,
that they could no longer win the war, the treatment meted out to the
prisoners became harsher day by day. A rumour that the Japanese
guards intended to kill their prisoners rather than hand them over to
an invading Allied force soon became to look uncomfortably like fact.
There was no doubt in the minds of those who survived, that had it
not been for the dropping of the atomic bombs on Hiroshima and

Nagasaki in August of that year, not one of them would have emerged from the camp alive.

When liberation finally came, William Phillips, once a heavily built, robust man, was an emaciated shadow of his former self, but with his spirit unbroken. He reached home in October 1945, where one of his first sad duties was to call on the wife of Second Officer Gordon Rowlandson and the mother of 18-year-old Apprentice Denys Matthews, both fellow Welshmen with a few words of comfort.

In a massive strike against Japanese ships sheltering in the Inland Sea in July 1945, American carrier-borne aircraft smashed the cruisers Aoba and Tone. Naomasa Sakonju and Haruo Mayazumi survived, but were later to pay for the massacre of the men of the Behar which they had instigated.

TEN

The brief sortie into the Indian Ocean by the Imperial Navy's 16th Squadron had proved to be a dismal failure. The Behar was Vice-Admiral Sakonju's one and only success, and earned herself the dubious distinction of being the last Allied merchantman to be sunk by an enemy surface raider in the Second World War. Having returned to their base, the Japanese heavy cruisers were never again to venture west of Sumatra.

The German and Japanese submarines, however, continued to wreak havoc in the Indian Ocean area. On 3 March, I-162, commanded by Lieutenant Y. Doi, sank the 7127-ton British steamer Fort McLeod 300 miles south-south-west of Ceylon, while four days later Kapitan-Leutnant Alfred Eick in U-510 sank the Norwegian motor vessel Tarifa, 7299 tons, 240 miles east of Socotra. The campaign was carried right to the Royal Navy's doorstep when, on the 9th, U-183, Kapitan-Leutnant Fritz Schneewind, torpedoed and set on fire the 6943-ton tanker British Loyalty lying at anchor off Adu Atoll. An American tanker, the 8298-ton H.D. Collier, was next to go, torpedoed in the Arabian Sea by I-26, Lieutenant-Commander T. Kusaka. The H.D. Collier went on fire and sank on the 16th, on which day RO-111, commanded by Lieutenant Naozo Nakamura, sent to the bottom in the Bay of Bengal the 3962-ton British troopship El Madina with heavy loss of life. In the first two weeks of March, then, the Allies lost in this area a total of 33,609 tons of priceless merchant shipping, a higher casualty rate than prevailed in the Atlantic at the time. The Admiralty would have prefered to introduce more convoys, but sufficient escorts were still not available.

Blissfully unaware of the increasing dangers in her path, the British cargo ship Nancy Moller sailed from Durban on 28 February, bound for Colombo with a full cargo of South African coal. The Nancy Moller, was even older than her late stable mate the Daisy Moller, sunk by RO-110 two months earlier. Built in Sunderland in 1907, she was a coal-burning steamer of 3916 tons gross; a maritime antique perhaps, but still capable of averaging 9 knots. She started life as the Rowena, and along the way changed her name to Norfolk, before ending up in the Far East with Mollers of Shanghai. Her crew was the usual mix of "China Coasters," British, Chinese and Indian, with inevitable White Russian emigre in the ranks. Her master, 31-year-old Captain James Hansen, of Norwegian extract, had been born and presently resided in Calcutta, Chief Officer Neil Morris hailed from Dunfermline, while Second Officer Shih Kao Chu and Third Officer Sui Yuang Chui were Hong Kong Chinese. The wireless room was in the hands of First Radio Officer John Goodson, also living in Calcutta, and Second Radio Officer Peter Quinn from Galway. Fifty-four-year-old, Russian-born Chief Engineer Danielovitch Tcherovsky had charge of the engine-room, and under him were Second Engineer Hsin Shing, Third Engineer Ah Ching and Fourth Engineer Kong Kwok Shun, all from Hong Kong. The Nancy Moller's 46 deck, engine-room and catering ratings were Lascars, while her wartime armament of one 12-pounder and five Oerlikons was manned and maintained by seven DEMS gunners, led by Able Seaman Gunlayer Dennis Fryers of Manchester.

In the less hazardous days of peace, the Nancy Moller would have taken the most direct route from Durban to Colombo, passing up through the Mozambique Channel between Madagascar and the African mainland, north of the Seychelles, and through the One-and-a-Half Degree Channel in the Southern Maldives. Things being what they were, the Admiralty had instructed Captain Hansen to pass south of Madagascar and take a long reach out into the Indian Ocean before turning north. This would add 200 or so miles to the passage, but with a cargo of coal what did a few more miles matter?

Chief Officer Neil Morris, right, with Captain and Mrs Hansen, taken at Government House, Bombay shortly before Nancy Moller sailed on her last voyage

There were many aboard the Nancy Moller who were puzzled at the nature of their cargo. Why, they asked, should they be taking coal across 3,800 miles of potentially hazardous ocean to Colombo when ample stocks were available in nearby India? This question was unlikely to be answered, but they all felt, from Hansen down, that putting the Nancy Moller under the coal tips at Durban had been nothing short of sacrilege. In her old trading days in the Far East she had carried mainly fine goods, cottons, silks and spices; clean, genteel cargoes. Undoubtedly the man least enamoured with the Nancy Moller's current cargo was her chief officer Neil Morris. The choking black dust that fouled the ship's paintwork during loading and permeated into every corner of her accommodation was burden enough, but for Morris it did not end there. A cargo of coal, inert and uninteresting though it may seem, carries with it considerable risks. Methane gas is given off, creating a danger of explosion, and the threat of spontaneous combustion is always present. Many a fine ship loaded with coal has been destroyed by a fire raging, undetected, deep in her holds. The chief officer of a coal carrier must therefore wage a constant battle of containment, with ventilation his only defensive weapon. Too much air entering the holds may cause fire or explosion, while insufficient ventilation has much the same effect. It is a very thin tightrope to walk, requiring meticulous trimming of ventilators and monitoring of temperatures in the holds. In the case of the Nancy Moller's passage through the heat of the tropics, the latter would be of vital importance, for in a mass of coal temperatures in excess of 77°F are critical. Many more mature and experienced men have developed stomach ulcers in the cause of the carriage of coal by sea. But Neil Morris, 25 years old and newly promoted to chief officer, had both youth and enthusiasm on his side. He would cope.

Having completed loading her odious cargo at The Bluff, Durban's coaling wharf carefully sited, well away from that fair city, the Nancy

Moller adjusted her compasses and tested her de-gaussing gear off the port before putting to sea. The voyage did not start well, for the weather once away from the coast was not as would have been expected in the southern summer. For the first week the deep-laden ship butted into strong north-easterly winds and rough seas, shipping water on deck, fore and aft. The trimming of the hold ventilators became a dangerous exercise, and with the decks constantly awash with sea water, taking temperatures of the cargo was out of the question. Neil Morris's worries had begun.

Neil McLeod Russell Morris, Chief Officer s.s. Nancy Moller

The first hint of impending trouble came not from the holds, but from a long way over the horizon. On 3 March a radio message was received from the Admiralty warning of a ship torpedoed directly in the Nancy Moller's intended path. This was the Fort MacLeod, sunk by I-162 some 350 miles south-south-west of Colombo. Captain Hansen took due note of the warning, but as his ship was then still to the south of Madagascar and barely able to maintain 6 knots in the adverse weather, he considered there was little to fear from the enemy for some time to come.

Seven days out of Durban, and clear of the south-eastern tip of Madagascar, the wind and sea fell away. Within 24 hours the Nancy Moller was bowling along at 9 knots under blue skies. As she progressed further to the north, the weather continued to improve, and so the spirits of those on board rose. Whatever dangers may lie ahead, it is difficult to be pessimistic when the sun is warm and the porpoises are leaping. Nevertheless, Hansen now followed the Admiralty's advice and began zig-zagging during daylight hours.

On 9 March, the Nancy Moller was south of Mauritius, with eleven days steaming to go to Colombo. Almost 3000 miles due east the hideous massacre of the Behar's innocents was about to take place, but here not a cloud marred the sky, and it is doubtful if any man aboard the Nancy Moller at that time would have believed the bestial level to which Japanese seamen could descend. They were to learn soon enough.

Late on the evening of the 17th the Nancy Moller, her passage continuing untroubled, was approaching the spot where 14 days earlier the Fort McLeod had been sunk. In just 36 hours she was due at Colombo, and it seemed the worst was over. Then, shortly after midnight, First Radio Officer John Goodson picked up a message from the Admiralty advising a sharp diversion to the east. Captain Hansen felt it highly unlikely that the submarine, which had sunk the Fort

McLeod was still in the area, but he could not afford to ignore the warning. Course was altered to due east and Hansen called on Chief Engineer Tcherovsky for more speed. There was a definite limit to what the old ship's engine could produce, but Tcherovsky, like all good chief engineers, had a little something up his sleeve. By 03.00 on the 18th, the log was recording 10 knots.

The Admiralty's advice proved disastrous. I-162 was in fact still in the area, and the diversion had been warranted, but further to the east was I-165, commanded by Lieutenant T. Shimizu. I-165, a pre-war submarine of 1635 tons displacement, achieved distinction in December 1941 by sighting and shadowing the Prince of Wales and Repulse, later to be sunk by torpedo bombers. Since then she had gone on to become one of the Imperial Navy's more successful boats. She ushered in 1944 well enough by sinking, on 16 January, the 10,286-ton British steamer Perseus in the Bay of Bengal, but there her good luck ran out. For the next two months she combed the seas around India and Ceylon with no reward. When, in the early hours of the morning of 18 March, the Nancy Moller came in sight, Lieutenant Shimizu took his boat to periscope depth and painstakingly stalked her until he had the advantage. At 08.30, he fired two torpedoes in quick succession.

The first torpedo tore into the Nancy Moller's port side, ripping open her thin plates in way of the engine-room and exploding with a crash that stunned her to a sudden halt. Second Officer Chu, had just returned to his cabin after taking morning sights. Dazed by the explosion, he struggled into his lifejacket and staggered back out into the alleyway. As he did so, the second torpedo struck immediately below the bridge, opening the Nancy Moller's empty deep tanks to the sea. By the time Chu reached the open deck, it was awash. A few seconds later the ship went down, taking him with her.

Caught unprepared, Chu swallowed great mouthfuls of salt water as he was dragged down into the green depths by the pull of the sinking ship. It seemed certain he must die, then, reluctantly, the Nancy Moller released her hold and Chu's lifejacket carried him to the surface before his lungs were completely filled.

Retching and gasping for breath, Chu found himself within reach of a lifebuoy, to which three other men were already clinging. The tiny ring of canvas-covered cork gave very little in the way of support for so many, but provided some reassurance in a world suddenly devoid of hope. The Nancy Moller, after tramping the oceans for 37 years, had gone to her last resting place in less than one minute, leaving behind her a sea thick with wreckage and covered with a film of coal dust. Nearby, several other survivors could be seen buoyed up by their lifejackets.

One of the men, with a hand on the same providential lifebuoy, was Chief Engineer Danielovitch Tcherovsky. Following a disturbed night spent nursing his hard-pressed engine, Tcherovsky had called at Captain Hansen's cabin, and was returning to his own quarters when the first torpedo struck. The Chief, who had been torpedoed on an earlier ship, was familiar with the drill. He immediately kicked off his shoes and slipped into his lifejacket, for he knew a ship loaded with coal would not float for long once her hull was pierced. As he was leaving his cabin at a run, he heard Hansen shout orders to lower the boats and saw Neil Morris rush past on his way to the boat deck to put the orders into effect. Tcherovsky noticed Morris was without his lifejacket and called him back, but the young chief officer was too intent on his mission to take notice. At that moment, another heavy explosion occurred and through the nearby open doors of the officers' dining saloon Tcherovsky saw the deck peel back like a banana skin and the sea well up from below like a seismic-driven tidal wave. Aware that the deep tanks, which provided the Nancy Moller's main reserve buoyancy were directly under the saloon, the Chief knew the ship did not have long to go.

When Tcherovsky reached the main deck, the Nancy Moller was listing heavily to port and he had great difficulty in keeping his feet. As he staggered awkwardly towards the boat deck ladder, a swell rolled over the bulwarks and swept him into the sea. He went under, but his lifejacket brought him quickly to the surface again and he found himself nudging the drifting lifebuoy. Some distance away he recognised Neil Morris and Third Officer Sui, who were without lifejackets and fighting to keep afloat.

The ship's gunners were on deck when the Nancy Moller was hit. For Gunlayer Dennis Fryers, who had his lifejacket to hand, it was a simple matter to leap into the sea when the deck dropped from under him. Able Seaman W. Lowe and Able Seaman A. Livermore had reached the boat deck and were in the act of freeing one of the lifeboats, when the sea rolled over them. Lowe swam to a life raft, where he was joined by Livermore and Able Seaman W. Noke and Able Seaman J. Morton. Three other rafts floated close by, two empty and one carrying Gunlayer Dennis Fryers, Second Engineer Shing, Engine-room Fitter Wong Chi May, and three Lascars.

Chu and Tcherovsky left the tenuous safety of the lifebuoy and hauled themselves aboard the keel of an upturned lifeboat, probably the boat Lowe and Livermore had been trying to release, when the ship went down. Chu could see no other boats in the immediate vicinity but all four of the Nancy Moller's life rafts had floated clear, and a large number of men were in the water. In spite of the dramatic suddenness of the sinking, it appeared that many of the crew had survived.

Further speculation was ended abruptly when I-165 surfaced not more than 50 yards off the boat. Chu judged her to be about 250 feet long, her paintwork was dark grey, and she mounted a gun of three or four inch calibre forward of her conning tower. As soon as her casings were above water, a number of khaki-clad figures tumbled out on deck carrying pistols and a light machine-gun. From the conning tower came the inevitable cry: "Where is Captain? Where is Chief Engineer?" Chu and Tcherovsky exchanged significant glances and slipped into the water, keeping the boat between themselves and the submarine.

The two men watched in silence as Lieutenant Shimizu, his questions ignored, manoeuvred alongside the nearest raft, on which were crouched Fryers, Shing, Wong Chi May, and the three Lascars. On another raft, the four DEMS ratings, Lowe, Livermore, Noke and Morton were also captive witnesses to what followed.

Addressing Fryers, Shimizu again demanded to know the whereabouts of the ship's captain and chief engineer, to which he received the standard reply, that both men had gone down with the ship. Fryers and his companions were ordered on board the submarine; the gun-layer being taken below. The remaining five men were forced to kneel down facing the bow, and to the absolute horror of the watching survivors, the Japanese showed their contempt for those who espoused the British cause. Hsin Shing was shot twice in the back and kicked overboard. He was not wearing a lifejacket and did not resurface. Wong Chi May was also shot in the back and kicked over the side. His lifejacket kept him afloat, but he was plainly badly wounded. It was now the turn of the three terrified Indians, who, perhaps because they were not even considered worthy of a bullet, were merely pushed contemptuously into the sea.

And so Shimizu's operation to blot out the Nancy Moller for ever, began. For the next ten minutes, I-165 slowly circled the area, nudging the wreckage aside and using her machine-guns indiscriminately, and to deadly effect. The survivors on the rafts were quick to jump overboard and hide behind their flimsy wooden craft, but for those caught drifting in the open there was no escape. Their blood mingled freely with the salty waters of the Indian Ocean.

Only when the sea was littered with lifeless bodies did the submarine cease fire and withdraw to the east, but it was another two hours before she was out of sight and the survivors of the massacre felt safe to come together. Remaining alive were, Second Officer Chu, Chief Engineer Tcherovsky, Fitter Wong Chi May, who was seriously injured, DEMS gunners Lowe, Livermore, Noke and Morton, and 25 Lascar seamen. A total of 32 of the Nancy Moller's original complement of 65 had died, including Captain James Hansen and Chief Officer Neil Morris, the majority of them gunned down by Shimizu's bullets, while struggling helplessly in the water. Gunlayer Dennis Fryers, a prisoner aboard I-165, had gone to a fate unknown.

Thirty-four-year-old Shih Kao Chu, being the only surviving deck officer, took charge of those remaining. He gathered together the four life rafts and distributed the 32 survivors, eight to a raft. The water and food tanks of one raft had been riddled by bullets and their contents ruined by sea water, and an attempt to rescue provisons from the upturned lifeboat failed. However, the three undamaged rafts contained sufficient food and water to sustain the survivors for a number of weeks, providing strict rationing was enforced.

Chu's plan for survival, which he discussed with the others, was in fact the only option open to them. As the two radio officers had been lost, there was no waying of knowing if an SOS had been sent out, but as the Nancy Moller had gone down so fast, this seemed highly unlikely. The south coast of Ceylon, lay only 250 miles to the north-east, but the wind was against them and there was little chance of using the clumsy square sails of the rafts. Under oars, it would be a long and exhausting pull, but there was no other choice. Having drifted for the rest of that day and night, they shipped oars and set off on the morning of the 19th, heading north.

They had not progressed far when the weather began to deteriorate, the wind freshening from the north-east, bringing with it an uncomfortable easterly swell. Under oars wielded by men who were already weak and demoralised, the heavy rafts soon became unmanageable in the wind and swell. Chu, on the leading raft, did his best to steer a reasonable course by the sun and stars, but he was constantly aware that, under the influence of the swell, they must be drifting steadily westwards. Occasional, heavy showers, proved to be a blessing, but they provided only brief respite from the searing heat of a sun that circled high in the sky, like a pulsating ball of burnished copper. At night the passing rain left them cold and shivering, longing for the return of the hot sun. Nature was applying a refined form of torture designed to break even the strongest among them. The Lascars, who far outnumbered the others, soon became troublesome, refusing to accept the food and water rationing, imposed by Chu. Fighting broke out and the rafts drifted apart. Hopes for survival dwindled.

On the evening of the 20th, the weather had become so bad that all pretence at rowing was abandoned and sea anchors were streamed in order to check the westerly drift, which was relentlessly taking the rafts away from the land. Throughout that night and all next day they drifted aimlessly, the distance between the rafts widening all the time. Then, shortly before sunset on the 21st, an aircraft was sighted to the west flying northwards. Smoke floats were set off and signal flags waved frantically, but the plane was obviously too far off to see them. Chu, ever the optimist, spread the word, that with the Nancy Moller being now overdue at Colombo, the aircraft had been sent out to look for them and more would follow. He was very likely wrong, but his confidence percolated through to the others and eyes began to search the horizon with renewed hope.

It was still only partly light when, at 05.30 on the 22nd, the fourth day adrift, a dark shadow was seen on the northern horizon. It could have been anything, even an enemy submarine, but desperation had set in on the rafts and caution went to the winds. Chu snatched up a torch and flashed out an urgent series of SOSs, which were acknowledged at once. The coming of full daylight revealed a ship bearing down on them. By 08.00, all the survivors were on board the British cruiser HMS Emerald. Four days later, they were landed at Port Louis, Mauritius.

HMS Emerald picks up survivors of Nancy Moller

For those who survived the sinking of the Nancy Moller the ordeal was over; for Gunlayer Dennis Fryers it had only just begun. Once aboard I-165, he was taken below at gunpoint and subjected to rigorous and continuous questioning, but to Shimizu's annoyance, Fryers did not talk. When the submarine reached Penang, the gunlayer was landed and thrown into solitary confinement, a punishment supplemented by a starvation diet and frequent brutal interrogations. After three months, his Japanese captors finally accepted they would get no information of value out of him and he was transferred to Singapore's notorious Changi gaol, where he was to spend the rest of the war enslaved in Emperor Hirohito's chain gangs. Dennis Fryers returned to Britain at the end of 1945 weighing just 84 lbs, another hollow-cheeked victim of Japan's attempt to conquer the East.

More survivors from the Nancy Moller

Fittingly, the Nancy Moller was I-165's last victim. At the end of August 1944 the submarine was badly damaged while attempting to supply Japanese troops on the Pacific island of Biak, but escaped to return to the Indian Ocean in the following month. Her fruitful days were finished, however. She sank no more Allied ships and was lost with all hands when attacked by US naval aircraft off Saipan on 27 June 1945. Lieutenant Shimizu was not in command of I-165 when she went down.

ELEVEN

The Great Australian Bight, a 1600-mile-long, south-facing bay that once formed Australia's interface with Antarctica, is the Biscay of the Antipodes. On the edge of the Roaring Forties and wide open to all the excesses of the inhospitable Southern Ocean, there are times when the Bight even succeeds in excelling the convulsions of its northern counterpart. It was so when, on the morning of 7 March 1944, the Dutch steamer Tjisalak sailed from Melbourne, bound for Colombo with a cargo of 6640 tons of bagged flour. As soon as she cleared the shelter of Port Philip Bay an ominous swell was encountered, and by the time Cape Otway was abeam, the heavily laden ship was feeling the full force of a westerly gale that was to persist for many days.

Built in Amsterdam in 1917 for the Royal Interocean Lines, the 5787-ton Tjisalak was a relic of an age when sea travel reigned supreme. Registered in Batavia, she had been employed exclusively in the Far East, and in addition to her cargo, was certified and equipped to carry 11 first class, 24 second class, 52 third class and 1380 steerage passengers, the latter packed like cattle on deck. In the years between the wars, the Tjisalak proved to be a most lucrative investment for her owners. Following the outbreak of the Second World War and the subsequent loss of her Dutch homeland, the steamer's fortunes were little affected until the Japanese moved into the Java Sea. She was then taken under the wing of the British Ministry of War Transport, escaping from Sourabaya only weeks before Admiral Sokichi's invasion fleet appeared off Java.

The following 18 months were memorable ones in the Tjisalak's long career. Rudely snatched from the balmy waters of the East, she was thrown into the holocust of the Battle of the Atlantic and performed exemplary service carrying war materials between America and the beleaguered British Isles. She bore a charmed life, for neither weather, U-boats nor Focke-Wulfs had harmed her during that testing time. When, late in 1943, with the changing pattern of the war, the Tjisalak returned to eastern waters, she was rusting and tired, but her oil-burning engines were still capable of driving her at a respectable 11 knots. As for her crew, they had become men hardened, in the furnace of war, beyond all recognition.

m.v. Tjisalak

Commanded by Captain C. Hen, the Tjisalak carried 11 Dutch and 3 British officers, 51 Hong Kong Chinese ratings and 10 British DEMS gunners. The senior officer on deck was Chief Officer Frits de Jong, and his opposite number in the engine-room Chief Engineer P.J. de Greeuw. The British were represented on deck by Second Radio Officer James Blears, Third Radio Officer J. Parker, and Apprentice M.A.F. Lister. Acting Petty Officer Alfred Arnold, with a team of six Royal Navy and four Maritime Regiment gunners, manned the ship's armament of one 4-inch anti-submarine gun, a multiple rocket launcher and four 20-mm Oerlikons.

As would be expected in those troubled times, the Dutch ship's passenger accommodation was far from full when she left Melbourne on her 18-day passage to the north. In her first class cabins were Mrs Verna Gorden-Britten, an American Red Cross nurse on her way to join her British army officer husband in Calcutta, three Australian commandos bound for the Burma front, and a British Army lieutenant. Travelling third class below decks were 22 Lascar seamen being repatriated to India following the loss of their ship. The total number on board the Tjisalak on leaving Melbourne was 103.

Rounding Cape Leeuwin on the morning of the 14th, the Tjisalak was already 24 hours behind schedule and the weather showed no signs of letting up. Captain Hen was becoming concerned, for he had left Melbourne with only four days reserve fuel in his bunkers. Colombo still lay 12 days steaming to the north and he could not afford to consume any more of this reserve. At the best of times, to run out of fuel while on a long ocean passage was a nightmare that might cost a shipmaster his job; in wartime it could cost him his ship and the lives of all on board. With this in mind, Hen called Chief Engineer de Greeuw to his cabin, and after some discussion, it was decided to reduce speed to 10 knots to conserve fuel. The odds were already being stacked against the once-lucky Tjisalak.

Further to the north the weather moderated, but another complication arose on the 16th, when the Tjisalak was some 500 miles to the north-west of Cape Leeuwin. A radio message from the Admiralty in Perth advised a change of course to the west, a long dogleg that would take the ship deep into the Indian Ocean and add almost 400 miles to the passage to Colombo. It is not known what prompted this radical deviation, but it could have been the Admiralty had got wind of the presence of Vice-Admiral Sakonju's ships operating off the Cocos Islands. Well-intentioned though the advice may have been – and it was advice that could not be ignored – it would serve to add to Captain Hen's problems by using up another one and a half day's fuel reserve.

Incredible though it may seem in retrospect, Perth Radio requested confirmation of the receipt of its diversionary message; even more incredibly, Hen sanctioned the breaking of radio silence for this to be done. A brief coded message might have caused no harm, but for two nights in succession the Tjisalak's operators spent many hours on the air vainly attempting to raise Perth. Durban Radio eventually answered their calls and agreed to pass their message to Perth. It appears not to have occurred to anyone on board that if Durban, 3000 miles away over the horizon, had heard their transmissions, other, less friendly ears might have been listening. The Tjisalak was courting more and more danger with every turn of her screw.

In answer to Captain Hen's fervent prayers, the weather was holding good, with clear skies, light winds and slight seas. He decided therefore to maintain an economical 10 knots until the ship was within 500 miles of Ceylon and entering the most dangerous waters. From then on he would press ahead at all possible speed, zig-zagging during the daylight hours and with lookouts doubled-up at all times. He was confident that, by the grace of God and the vigilance of her crew, the

Tjisalak would reach Colombo on the 28th unharmed and with a small reserve of oil remaining in her bunkers.

The danger zone to the south of Ceylon was entered in the early hours of Sunday the 26th. It was a fine morning, with a light westerly wind and a slight sea running. Hen was on the bridge early, intending to increase speed and commence zig-zagging at daybreak, which would be around 06.00. Not wishing to interfere with the navigation of the ship, which was in the capable hands of Chief Officer de Jong and Fourth Officer Visser, Hen climbed the vertical ladder to the open upper bridge, to find he had been preceded by one of the Australian commando passengers, an early riser intent on seeing the sun come up. The two men exchanged pleasantries. It was a peaceful scene, the measured thump of the Tjisalak's engine, muted, as the shadows of the night slowly melted before the coming sun and the ship around them began to take on a tangible form. Below them, in the port wing of the navigation bridge, a duffel-coated DEMS gunner idly swung the long barrel of his Oerlikon around the emerging horizon, alert and ready. In the opposite wing, the Chinese lookout man stood motionless, watching the slowly hardening horizon, but with his thoughts reaching far beyond it. Turning aft, Hen saw the vague outlines of two more gunners pacing the 4-inch gun platform. From the galley funnel a thin trail of blue-grey smoke drifted to starboard, indicating the cooks were brewing the first coffee of the day.

Frits de Jong finished working up his morning sights and plotted the ship's position on the chart as 02° 30'S 78° 40'E. It was exactly 05.45 when he stepped out of the chartroom. A frantic cry of "Hard-a-port! Hard-a-port!" came from above, followed by a loud thump as Captain Hen took the fastest route down, from the upper bridge. De Jong reached the port wing in time to see twin streaks of bright phosphorescence racing neck and neck towards the ship from a point ten degrees forward of the beam. Before the Tjisalak's bows had begun to swing in response to her rudder, the two torpedoes struck her abaft the bridge with an enormous double explosion that lifted her, bodily, out of the water. Oil from her punctured fuel tanks gushed skywards, covering the bridge with black slime, the engine came to an abrupt halt, all lights went out, and she took a heavy list to port. At the same time, inevitably, the main and emergency wireless aerials came crashing down, thwarting the efforts of First Radio Officer Vleeschhouwer, who had already begun to transmit a distress.

Second Officer Jan Dekker, having been on watch from midnight to 04.00, was sound asleep in his cabin when the torpedoes struck. At first, he lay half way between sleep and awakening, unable to grasp what had happened. Then, when the Tjisalak lurched to port and did not return to the upright, the message struck home. Coming fully awake and alert to the danger, it took only a matter of seconds for him to throw on a few clothes, snatch up his lifejacket and vacate the cabin.

As well as being the ship's navigator, Dekker also had a subsidiary wartime role as gunnery officer, and his first reaction to the emergency was to make his way aft to the 4-inch gun, where the DEMS gunners should be taking up their action stations. He found the starboard alleyway of the accommodation in darkness and awash with oil; this combined with the heavy list made his progress aft painfully slow. When he eventually reached the outside deck, he walked into a shambles. Wreckage lay everywhere; derricks and winches were an unrecognisable mass of tangled metal, No.3 hold had lost its hatchboards and beams, and clouds of steam poured from the stokehold entrance abaft the hold. Overall lay a ghostly coating of flour, blown from the hold by the force of the explosion. In the grey light of the dawn, the area between the bridge and the engineers' accommodation block had the appearance of the crater of a recently erupted volcano.

The Tjisalak had partially righted herself, ending up with a 15-degree list, but she still had way on her, and with her helm jammed hard to port, was running in tight circles like a wounded animal. There was no doubt that she was sinking fast, and Captain Hen had already given the order to abandon ship. Frightened and bewildered by the catastrophic event that brought them early from their bunks, the Chinese crew were near to panic, but under the steadying hand of their officers, they assembled on the boat deck. The two lifeboats on the port side, which were only a few feet above the water, were launched without difficulty, but owing to the list, only one of the starboard side boats could be lowered.

Not aware that the ship was being abandoned, Jan Dekker reached the poop to find the 4-inch gun's crew standing-to, they too had failed to hear the call to take to the boats. At their stations around the already loaded gun were Petty Officer Arnold, Able Seaman Fred Mather, Able Seaman Patrick O'Brien, Able Seaman Fred Drewery, Able Seaman Albert Fieldhouse, Able Seaman Fred Perry, and Bombardier John Burns. Second Radio Officer James Blears, having discharged his primary duty by stowing the portable radio and a rifle and ammunition in the small lifeboat on the poop, was standing by to assist with the gun.

As the first rays of the rising sun spread their orange glow over the eastern horizon, the loud rattle of an Oerlikon broke the silence and the startled gunners saw tracers arcing seawards from the port wing of the bridge. The shells were directed at a flurry of broken water about 1000 yards off the quarter, in which could be seen the twin periscopes of a surfacing submarine. The Oerlikon gunner was Apprentice Peter Bronger who, although the lifeboats had pulled away from the ship, stayed behind to alert the 4-inch crew. Having succeeded in his aim, Bronger then dived overboard and swam to the nearest boat.

Dekker, as officer-in-charge of the 4-inch, was now faced with the choice of joining battle with the submarine or abandoning ship, as the others had so obviously done. But with more and more of the submarine appearing, and with the gun loaded and pre-set for 1000 yards, the opportunity to strike back was too good to miss. Dekker gave the order to open fire. The time was 05.48: three minutes had elapsed since the torpedoes struck home.

It was a far cry from the gun drills they had carried out in Melbourne harbour before sailing. The Tjisalak was still under way, and with her helm jammed hard over, continued to turn to port, making sighting difficult. The ship's list was still considerable and depressing the gun sufficiently was a problem, but when the 4-inch thundered and recoiled for the first time, the shell fell only a little short and in line with the enemy. The second and third shots landed even closer; so close the submarine decided to submerge again. This was beautiful, precison firing, and Dekker and his British gunners, surging with enthusiasm, had every reason to be proud of their efforts.

Dekker subdued the cheering that broke out on the sloping gun platform, and as the ship continued to swing slowly, kept the 4-inch trained on the area of disturbed water where the enemy had dived. Several tense minutes passed, then the periscopes reappeared with a rush, quickly followed by the conning tower and casing of the submarine. Firing was recommenced and four more shots were got away before the gun came up against the restraining stops, fitted to prevent shells striking the superstructure of the ship. Dekker was forced to order the cease fire. The Tjisalak, still turning to port, had taken the submarine out of their line of sight.

It was now 06.00, and the sun had broken free of the horizon to bathe the crippled ship in its warm rays. But as the sun rose, so the list increased, until it reached 50 degrees and it was impossible to stand upright on the gun platform, over which the sea was now lapping.

Dekker realised the Tjisalak's end was very near and ordered his men over the side. The order came not a second too soon. As the men surfaced and swam away from the ship, she rolled on her beam ends, lifted her bows in the air, and sank, fortunately for those in the water, with very little suction.

Shortly before going over the side, Radio Officer James Blears had the presence of mind to release the falls of the small poop lifeboat, which due to the list was then touching the water. The boat floated clear as the ship sank and the gun's crew gratefully hauled themselves aboard. The oars were shipped and they rowed towards the other boats, huddled together some half a mile away. When they reached them, they found two of the three boats damaged and leaking. However, with the exception of three Chinese engine-room ratings killed by the explosion, the remainder of the Tjisalak's passengers and crew were safe.

Some of the ship's life rafts surfaced after she went down and could now be seen floating amongst the pitiful mess of wreckage marking her last resting place. As these rafts contained food and water, which might soon be sorely needed, Second Officer Jan Dekker, who had charge of the handiest boat, was detailed to salvage what he could. Blears and the gunners bent their backs to the oars and the small boat soon reached the nearest raft. They were making preparations to board it when the submarine came to the surface within 100 yards of the other boats. Her long, grey-painted hull was full of menace.

The Japanese submarine I-8 had the distinction of being one of the Imperial Navy's most travelled ships. Built shortly before the outbreak of war, she had cruised extensively in the Pacific, taking part in all the major campaigns from Pearl Harbor on. In July 1943, she sailed from Penang on a marathon voyage that was to take her around the Cape of Good Hope and northwards, 6400 miles to Germany. She returned by the same route, with every available space in her hull packed with war materials, vital to Japan. The 30,000-mile round voyage lasted almost five months and must surely rank as one of the longest and most hazardous ever undertaken by a conventional submarine. The 1955-ton boat had a surface speed of 23 knots, carried a crew of 80 and was armed with two 14-cm guns, one 22-mm cannon and 20 torpedoes. She also carried a small, one-man seaplane, used for spotting purposes. But, in spite of being so equipped and tested, I-8, under various commanders, had been singularly unsuccessful, having failed to sink a single enemy ship of consequence in all her wide voyaging. After combing the Indian Ocean for six weeks without a kill, I-8's current commander, Lieutenant-Commander Tatsunoseke Ariizumi, must surely have been overjoyed on sighting the fully-loaded Tjisalak. She was a prize worthy of the long wait.

Jan Dekker watched from afar as a number of men emerged on the deck of the submarine and began making urgent gestures for the lifeboats to come alongside. More figures appeared in the conning tower and there was the usual demand for the captain to reveal himself. Dekker identified the owner of the lisping, strident voice as Japanese.

At first there was no answer from the boats, Captain Hen no doubt debating the wisdom of delivering himself into the hands of the enemy. But when the demand was repeated again and again, with the caller's voice rising to an angry screech, Hen identified himself and was told to bring his boat alongside the submarine. Dekker now concluded it would be wise to withdraw to a safer distance and ordered the gunners to take up their oars again. As they moved stealthily away, Captain Hen was seen to board the submarine, followed by the others in his boat. When they were on the casings, the Japanese moved among them and a group consisting of Hen, Third Officer Koning, Chief Engineer de Greeuw, Second Engineer Graler, Fourth Engineer

Wittenaar, Verna Gorden-Britten and two other passengers, were taken to the forward hatch and disappeared below.

The shouting began again and the other two lifeboats were ordered alongside. Meanwhile, Dekker urged his rowers on and gained a few more yards before the calls for them to return became too insistent to ignore. They could have carried on rowing, but there was really nowhere for the boat to go, and Dekker feared the Japanese would lose patience and open fire on them. Reluctantly, he swung the tiller over and the boat came around in a wide circle to head towards the submarine. As it did so, the Japanese sailors began shouting excitedly, some scanning the skies with binoculars. For one glorious moment Dekker thought an aircraft might be coming to their rescue, but the skies remained empty.

As the small boat skirted the stern of the submarine, Dekker took a mental note that her paintwork was in excellent condition. Her conning tower was large and had twin guns mounted forward of it, each of which Dekker judged to be larger than the Tjisalak's 4-inch. It also struck him as strange that, for a craft designed to spend much of its time under water, the submarine had a great deal of brasswork on deck, including a large bell, all of which was brightly polished. He concluded cynically her crew must have little else to occupy their time while on patrol. As to the men in sight, they were all smartly dressed in clean khakis and seemed very young, but a certain lack of discipline was indicated by the way they constantly argued amongst themselves.

Dekker's benign observations were brought to a rude end when the boat was laid alongside and he stepped warily aboard the enemy ship at the head of his eight-man crew. They were ordered forward of the conning tower, where Japanese guards armed with an assortment of Tommy guns, rifles and swords searched them roughly, relieving them of watches, rings, and anything else of value. They were then forced at gunpoint to squat on the deck alongside the Tjisalak survivors already on board. A few moments later, the lifeboats were cut adrift and the submarine's diesels roared into life. Dekker found the situation difficult to assess, but could not help entertaining hopes that the intention was to carry them away as prisoners, perhaps later transferring them to a surface vessel.

The possibility became somewhat remote when Dekker heard Captain Hen's voice from the conning tower. The captain was clearly under great stress and being interrogated in a very forceful manner. His protest, "No. I don't know! I don't know!" sounded like a cry from the heart. Instinctively, Dekker turned his head to look aft and consequently became the target for abuse. "Don't look back! Don't look back!" a Japanese guard screamed. "If you look back you will be shot." The guard's frenzied screams started a movement of panic amongst the Chinese squatting on the deck, one of whom got to his feet and fell overboard. The guards opened fire on the unfortunate seaman as he drifted astern. Whether or not he was hit Dekker could not tell, but he feared the killing was about to start.

He had concluded rightly. The Japanese began selecting their victims, beginning with the Europeans. Two of the DEMS gunners were first to be dragged aft. Dekker did not dare to look back, but he heard the shots and guessed what was happening. Chief Officer de Jong and Fifth Engineer Berger were next to go; Frits de Jong, weighing 280 lbs and 6ft 6ins tall, dwarfed the guards who were beating him with their gun butts. Another fusilade of shots rang out when they disappeared abaft the conning tower.

Then came Jan Dekker's turn. He was hauled unceremoniously to his feet, his lifejacket was ripped off and he was bundled aft at gunpoint. He tried to hold back, but was told he would be shot if he resisted. When he came abreast of the conning tower, he felt a tremendous blow to the side of his head. He staggered, and as he did so, glimpsed another Jap swinging at him with a sledge hammer. He tried to duck, but the hammer caught him a glancing blow on the right temple. Dazed, he crashed to the deck and looked up to find himself staring at the barrel of a rifle. The look in the eyes of the man behind the gun was enough to convince Dekker he was about to die. With a desperate twist of his body, he rolled off the casing into the sea and dived deep.

Although he was in considerable pain from the blows to his head, Dekker remained submerged for as long as his lungs would allow. Overhead he heard the hiss of bullets striking the water and the beat of the submarine's propellors as it passed close by. Twice he came to the surface for air, and each time he was forced under again by a hail of bullets. When he came up for the third time, gasping painfully and with his strength ebbing fast, the submarine was some way ahead and the firing had stopped. Either the Japanese considered him to be dead, or they had turned to easier targets.

This was no time to speculate. Dekker struck out powerfully, anxious to put as much distance as possible between the enemy submarine and himself. He swam on and on, drawing on all his reserves of strength, then – it may have been an hour, it may have been two hours later – when he was all but exhausted, he reached a piece of floating wreckage. This kept him afloat until he came upon an upturned lifeboat. He swam to the boat and dived under it, surfacing in the air pocket beneath. For the time being at least, he was safe and out of sight, should the Japanese submarine return.

Second Radio Officer James Blears was one of a group of prisoners near the bows of I-8. When he saw the Tjisalak's Dutch officers being taken aft he realised the time for positive action was at hand. The shouts, the screams and the shots that followed gave him the necessary motivation and he tensed himself to go over the side, but before he could act, a Lascar seaman, who must have been thinking along the same lines, jumped up and dived overboard. The Indian came to the surface thrashing the water in blind panic, but he had not gained more than a few feet of freedom when a machine-gun opened up and the bullets slammed into his body.

Blears was stunned and sickened, unable to move. He was still in a daze when the killing began in earnest. Japanese guards carrying swords moved in amongst the remaining Lascars, who were forced to their knees and beheaded one by one. It was a scene of absolute bestiality, but the screams for mercy and the blood paled into comparative insignificance when Blears saw the cameraman leaning over the edge of the conning tower. The Japanese were actually filming the atrocity!

As he crouched fascinated and horrified by the awful events he was witnessing, Blears was hit with the flat of a sword and rough hands dragged him aft to the conning tower. At the foot of the tower he found several DEMS gunners being bound with their hands behind their backs. One gunner, who had obviously been pushed beyond the limits of his British phelgm, lashed out at his captors as Blears approached. Showing as much compassion as he would for a wild beast, one of the Japanese slashed at the angry gunner with his sword, splitting open his skull and back, before kicking him overboard like a bloodsoaked rag doll.

Second Radio Officer James Blears, 1989

When Blears found himself being tied, he had the presence of mind, and the strength – he was an amateur wrestler – to strain against the bonds so that his wrists were not bound tightly. He was then joined to Apprentice Peter Bronger by a short length of rope and the guards laid into them with the flat of their swords, driving them past the conning tower towards the stern of the submarine. Blears was in the lead and had a premonition that death was waiting for them on the other side of the tower. He was therefore prepared for what happened next. As they stumbled clear of the tower, they were faced by two Japanese, one armed with a sword, the other with a sledgehammer, and both poised to strike. Blears ducked the sword blow, kicked out at the man with the hammer, and threw himself overboard to starboard, taking Bronger with him. When underwater Blears was able to wrench his hands free and struck out to clear the submarine's threshing propellors as he and the young apprentice, still joined by the rope, drifted aft.

The Japanese opened fire, the bullets churning up the water around the two men. Blears dived, doing his best to pull Bronger under with him, but the boy was heavy and appeared to have been hit. When he came to the surface again, Blears looked back at the submarine to witness yet another bizarre scene. Three laughing Japanese sailors, seated comfortably in chairs, were firing at them with rifles, much as if they were on an organised game shoot – which of course they were. Blears trod water, unable to believe his eyes, but when a machine-gun opened up from the conning tower, he dived deep, dragging the inert Bronger with him.

Blears continued to porpoise with his heavy burden, until at last the bullets ceased to come. The Japanese had either tired of their murderous game, or they were out of range. He trod water again and examined Bronger, who was still secured to his right wrist by the rope. The apprentice was unconscious and bleeding profusely from a wound in his back. He had most certainly caught a burst of machine gun fire and seemed near to death. However, Blears was reluctant to leave the boy and for the next hour supported him as he swam determinedly away from the submarine. Only when he was sure Peter Bronger was beyond help did Blears untie the rope and leave him.

In his youth, 21-year-old James Blears was selected for the British Olympics swimming team. The war prevented him competing, but all the rigorous training he had undergone now came to his aid. Using a distinctive group of clouds on the horizon to give him direction, he struck out towards where he thought the Tjisalak's empty lifeboats might be. Although the sea was smooth, there was a heavy swell running and his progress was slow and hard-won. It was late afternoon when, at the end of his physical and mental endurance, a larger than usual swell lifted Blears high and all his efforts were rewarded. He was 50 yards off an area of floating wreckage, within which drifted three lifeboats and two rafts.

It was like coming home, for the first floating object Blears reached was the oak card table around which he had enjoyed so many games with his fellow officers in the watches below. Then he heard a cry from one of the rafts and swam towards it. Lying spreadeagled on the raft was Chief Officer Frits de Jong, bleeding from a bullet wound in his head, but still conscious. While Blears dressed his wound with sulphur powder and bandages from the raft's locker, the chief officer told his story.

When De Jong was taken aft by the Japanese along with Berger, he was forced to look on while the junior engineer was shot in the head and dumped overboard. Berger, a very likeable young man, had escaped from German occupied Holland only a few months previously, and it made de Jong extremely angry to see him die in such an ignominious way. But the chief officer, big man though he might be, was surrounded by armed Japanese and was powerless. He was pushed and jostled aft to where his executioner waited with cocked revolver. De

Jong stopped beside the man and looked down at him with contempt, expecting to be shot like a dog, as Berger had been. The Japanese, with a wave of his pistol ordered him to keep moving aft. When he arrived at the extreme end of the deck and felt the vibrations of the propellors under his feet, de Jong heard a bang, his head seemed to explode and he lost consciousness.

Although he was not aware of it, Frits de Jong's height had saved him from death. The much smaller Japanese executioner had been obliged to fire upwards at an angle, with the result that the bullet only grazed de Jong's scalp. He was doubly fortunate in that he was still wearing a lifejacket, which kept him afloat until he found the raft five hours later.

About 20 minutes after Blears boarded the raft they were joined by Third Engineer Spuybroek, who had had a similar escape, throwing himself overboard before the Japanese could shoot him. All the bullets that came after him missed and he later found a discarded lifejacket, which kept him afloat.

With Spuybroek's help, Blears inspected the boats drifting nearby. In one was a portable lifeboat radio, which was immediately transfered to the largest of the boats. The injured de Jong was ferried over to this boat and all food and water collected from the other boats. By the time they had salvaged everything of use to them it was almost dark. The mast was stepped, and they were about to hoist the sail when they heard shouts. Second Officer Jan Dekker and a Lascar seaman named Dhange were swimming towards them.

After half an hour or so in the air bubble beneath the upturned lifeboat, Dekker became restless and surfaced to look around. He climbed on to the keel of the boat and scanned the horizon. There was no sign of the submarine, but three or four miles away he saw wreckage and two lifeboats floating right side up. He also became aware of a number of large sharks circling his boat. The thought of what these brutes would have done to him if they had found him sheltering underneath the boat brought him out in a cold sweat.

As he contemplated the sharks, Dekker caught sight of a man outside the circle of sharks and swimming towards him. He splashed at the water and shouted until he was hoarse, and succeeded in scaring off the sharks while Dhange, one of the Tjisalak's Lascar passengers, reached the boat. When Dekker hauled him aboard, Dhange was exhausted and bleeding from two deep wounds to the back of his neck. He had narrowly escaped decapitation by a Japanese sword.

When the Lascar had rested for a while, Dekker decided it was time to make a bid for the other lifeboats, which at least were floating right side up. Keeping a wary eye on the sharks, he dived under the boat again and came up with an oar. Had the boat been upright, he would have succeeded in sculling towards the other boats, but balanced on the keel and without a fulcrum for his oar, he was attempting the impossible. Forward movement was negligible, but while Dekker was standing on the keel he discovered he could see men in one of the distant boats. Waving and shouting produced no response from the men, and no matter which way Dekker tried to apply his oar, he could not move the heavy boat against the swells. There was only one alternative left. Dhange was persuaded to take to the water again, and creating as much commotion as possible to keep the sharks at bay, the two men set out to swim to the other boat.

The swim was long and arduous, and it was almost dark by the time Blears and Spuyboek spotted Dekker and his companion and went to their rescue. When they were hauled aboard, Dekker found Frits de Jong bravely seated at the tiller, but the chief officer was in no condition to take charge. As next in line of seniority, the responsibility therefore rested on Dekker's shoulders. His first priority was to apply his elementary knowledge of first aid to the treatment of the wounds of de Jong and Dhange. Having done his best, he turned his mind to the preparations to be made before they tackled the 500-mile voyage to Ceylon – for this was what they must do if they were to survive. His preparations were thorough. Assisted by Blears and Spuybroek, Dekker set about stripping the other boats. By the time they had finished, they had on board 10 tanks of fresh water, sufficient food for two months, two compasses, two sets of sails, and extra axes and ropes.

The lifeboat's seams had opened up through long months spent in the chocks under the hot sun and it was leaking badly, but this was a disadvantage they could live with. The sails were hoisted without more delay, and with Dekker at the tiller steering north, the voyage commenced. Only then did the five men, sole survivors of the Tjisalak's original complement of 103, begin to piece together the full horror of the day. Dhange, the last man to leave the Japanese submarine alive, told how he had seen Captain Hen killed with a sword in the conning tower, but had no knowledge of the fate of those taken below. It was assumed the four men, de Greeuw, Koning, Graler and Wittenaar must have met a similar end, and as for the American nurse Verna Gorden-Britten, it seemed best not to speculate. In fact, one of I-8's crew, giving evidence for the Allies at the War Crimes Trials held in Tokyo after the war, testified that the woman had been taken up on deck that night and shot.

Dhange described in detail how, when the Japanese had slaughtered all but about twenty of the prisoners on deck, those remaining were roped together and pushed overboard to be towed behind the submarine like a grotesque fishing line baited with kicking, screaming human beings. The Japanese then deliberately dived the submarine, dragging the drowning wretches under. Dhange, who was the last man on the towrope, succeeded in freeing himself as he went under, and so escaped death.

There was no time to indulge in grief or anger; that would come later. The short tropical twilight had turned quickly to night, and with the darkness came heavy rain. As the boat was already partly water-logged, the rain was an added burden. Throughout that night, the five survivors, three of them injured, took turns to bail and stand watch at the tiller. The next day passed without incident, a day spent languishing in the burning sun, reliving the horrors they had endured. They were all in poor shape and reaction to their ordeal was setting in. James Blears, who had had a particularly rough time, was near to collapse, while Frits de Jong's condition was deteriorating steadily.

Another night passed, and on the morning of the 28th, Dekker judged the Japanese submarine to be out of range and it would soon be safe to use the portable radio transmitter. Only Blears was able summon up enough strength to climb the mast and rig an aerial, an operation which took an exasperatingly long time. When the job was at last done, the survivors opened a tin of peaches in celebration and prepared to wait for darkness, when wireless reception would be at its best.

In the afternoon, Spuybroek took over the watch at the tiller, while the others found what shade they could and tried to sleep. Jan Dekker was still awake an hour later, when he heard Spuybroek let out a frightened shout. The engineer, who had turned deathly pale, was gesturing astern. He had sighted the conning tower of a submarine.

This was a bitter blow to the survivors. It could only mean their Japanese persecutor had returned to finish his bloody work. This time they had nowhere to hide, nowhere to run to. Half an hour passed, while they crouched low in the boat, once again imagining they were near to death. Then another miracle was added to the list of those that had delivered them from the hands of the Japanese. The conning tower grew into the bridge of a ship, and a hysterical, but ineffectual, scramble to find a means of attracting attention began. Order was quickly restored when the ship opened fire with a heavy gun.

With shells falling all around the boat, Dekker recognised the ship as an American-built Liberty-type merchantman and assumed she must be a Japanese prize being used as a surface raider. There could be no other explanation for the attack on a defenceless lifeboat. He advised his companions to strip off what few rags of clothing they possessed and be ready to go over the side. The dreadful nightmare was about to begin all over again.

The ship was quite close, but was altering away from the boat, still firing. Dekker lowered the lifeboat's sail and the Liberty's gun fell silent. The survivors breathed again, but their hopes were dashed when the ship opened fire on them with a machine-gun. They were about to take to the water when the firing ceased and boarding ladders came rattling down the side of the ship, which was now only a few hundred yards off. Europeans could be seen lining the rails, and the men in the lifeboat knew their suffering was at an end. Naked but caring not, they reached for their oars.

Dekker was first to reach the deck of the James A. Wilder. Unfortunately, his welcome aboard was bizarre. A pistol was thrust into his back and he was frogmarched to the bridge, his protests unheeded. There he was confronted by an angry American captain, who demanded to know why the survivors had not fired rockets or made any distress signals. Only when Dekker explained the circumstances prevailing in the boat did Captain Lunt simmer down and apologise for the gunfire. He explained that he had 40 passengers on board, including a number of women, and having mistaken the lifeboat for the conning tower of an enemy submarine, had taken swift defensive action. In the circumstances, his behaviour was understandable, but it almost cost the lives of the only men to survive the sinking of the Tjisalak.

The survivors were landed at Colombo on 30 March, and what happened to them then can only be given credence by the reader by quoting verbatim part of Second Officer Jan Dekker's statement made to the Admiralty on 28 December 1944.

We landed at 20.00 and walked to the N.C.S.O's offices where we had to climb five flights of stairs, a very difficult feat for two of the men, who had bad feet and legs. Lieut. Travers telephoned and after half an hour got in touch with a Shipping Agent to whom he reported 5 Dutch survivors. This Agent asked the name of the ship and Lt. Travers said he was not allowed to give him that information over the telephone, whereupon the Agent said he could do nothing for us, but finally agreed to ring up in 5 minutes when he found out the name of our ship. Lieut. Travers still refused to give him the ship's name and rang up the RN Hospital. They enquired whether we were Royal Navy personnel, and on being told that we were Merchant Seamen they said they were very sorry but they could not help, as their Instructions would not allow them to do anything for us. Lieut. Travers then rang the General Hospital and after a lot of arguing about who should pay for an ambulance to fetch us, we agreed to pay for it with our own money. Finally, at about 23.00, the ambulance arrived, we found it was in an absolutely filthy condition, but as we were in urgent need of some kind of medical attention, we decided we had better go in it to the hospital.

On arriving at the Hospital at about 23.30, we enquired for the Doctor, who proved to be a native. I told him we needed medical attention and wished to be put up for the night. A nun came along and took off the bandages from my head and feet, she said that my wounds were already badly infected. The Doctor then said, "There is no room in this hospital, except in the non-paying ward, and as I don't suppose you want to stay there, what are you going to do?" The Lascar said he would stay, and the Chief Officer was by now so thoroughly exhausted that he said he would also stay. I asked the nun to replace my bandages, but she said that as I was not going to have any treatment at that hospital she could not do anything further, and walked away. I made the Doctor bring her back, and after some further argument she re-bandaged my head and feet.

As we were leaving the hospital we met a British Chief Petty Officer who asked if he could do anything for us. I told him our story and that we were survivors requiring medical attention and a bed for the night. He said he would try to contact the Commander of the RN Hospital, which was only on the opposite side of the road. The Radio Officer walked across to the RN Hospital and requested to see the Commanding Officer. We explained our case to him, he said he was very sorry but he could do nothing for us, all he could do would be to report it to the authorities. The Chief Petty Officer, who came back with us, said that he could do nothing further and that he was ashamed of the Royal Navy.

We finally telephoned to the Dutch Naval Authorities, who were just as much to blame. I asked them to send a car for us and they said they would do their best; eventually we went to the Goldface (Galle Face?) Hotel. It was now 02.00 on the 31st, and on arriving at this Hotel we were told by a native night porter that there were no rooms available. However, he said he would fix up something for us, and arranged for us to sleep on a settee in the ballroom, but we had to promise to be up by 07.00 and say nothing to the Manager. He turned on the fans, and in the morning brought us tea and toast, for which he paid himself, we also had a bath and a shave, and this was the first kind action we received at Colombo.

It is to the eternal shame of those responsible in Colombo that such hideous indignity should have been heaped upon these five brave men, the only survivors of the Tjisalak massacre. They had endured so much at the hands of their enemies, yet when they thought they were at last among friends, they found themselves treated like lepers. Only a poor native porter, who was himself a victim of an unjust system, showed compassion and offered succour. One can only hope that one day this lowly and unknown Samaritan received a just reward for his kindness.

TWELVE

By the winter of 1940, as the Battle of the Atlantic moved towards its awesome crescendo, a crisis of immense proportions faced British merchant shipping. Up to 100 ships a month, three ships a day, were falling to the U-boats alone, a haemorrhage not even the great shipyards of the North East of England and the Clyde could hope to stem. The need was for a standard design, deep-sea ship, capable of carrying a large amount of cargo with maximum fuel economy, to be built quickly and in large numbers. If this need could not be fulfilled, then the flow of war materials and food coming across the Atlantic from the USA and Canada would be eventually choked off and Britain, the last remaining bastion of freedom remaining in Europe, would fall.

Armed with a design based on a Sunderland tramp built in the late 1930s, British envoys crossed the Atlantic, and from their negotiations was born the 7000-ton, prefabricated, all-welded "Liberty" ship. The Liberty differed from the Sunderland tramp only in that the Americans sited all accommodation amidships in one single block, and adopted water-tube boilers fired by oil, rather than the traditional coal-fired Scotch boiler. The project was put in the dynamic hands of Henry J. Kaiser, a construction engineer who had no previous involvement in shipbuilding, but was a trail-blazing entrepreneur in the best American style. Kaiser set in motion a shipbuilding programme the like of which the world had never seen before. Using mass production techniques similar to those adopted by the car industry, 18 US shipyards from Maine to California started work around the clock, using hastily trained labour, including many thousands of women. The first Liberty took six months to build, but by September 1942, they were coming off the stocks at the rate of two every day, the average time from keel to delivery being only four weeks. The miracle came none too soon, for by then, with the USA herself forced into war by Japan, Allied merchant ship losses were running at 130 a month.

The Liberty, powered by a triple-expansion steam engine, which gave it a speed of 11 knots, was said to have been built to be sunk, having a projected lifetime of six months. If a Liberty achieved this age, it was argued, then it would have carried a great deal of vital cargo across the Atlantic, and so served its primary purpose. That is not to say the Liberty was shoddily built. Like its British antecedent, it proved to be a tough, dependable workhorse, its only serious fault being it had insufficient draught in the ballast condition. A Liberty flying light presented such a huge expanse of hull above the waterline it often became unmanageable in strong winds. Between 1941 and 1945, no less than 2770 of these ships were built, the majority of them going to the American Merchant Marine, which used them in all theatres of the war. Many were sunk, of course, but contrary to predictions, hundreds of these tough, barge-shaped ships lived on for years after the war, giving excellent service to shipowners and crews alike. The last of the Liberties went to the breaker's yard as late as 1975, a fitting tribute to Henry J. Kaiser and his teams of housewife and shopgirl riveters.

The Richard Hovey was a Liberty ship out of the Portland, Maine yard, a typical product of Henry Kaiser's production lines. Of 7176 tons gross, she was owned by the US War Shipping Administration and operated by the Sprague Steamship Company of Boston, Massachusetts. She left Bombay on the evening of 27 March 1944, bound for the USA via Aden, having on board a mixed cargo of tea, jute, hemp, gunnies and US Army personal effects, totalling 3,600 tons. Commanded by Captain Hans Thorsen, a Norwegian-born US citizen, her complement of 71 included an Armed Guard Unit of 28 under Lieutenant Harry C. Goudy, USNR, an Army Cargo Security Officer, Lieutenant F.W. Anderson, and one passenger, Coxswain A.F. Schwalfowski, USN.

In British merchant ships, defence was given a relatively low priority, usually taking the form of a few First World War vintage guns manned by a handful of trained DEMS gunners, backed up by the ship's crew. The US Navy, turning a convenient blind eye to the discredited Geneva Convention, took a more aggressive view. The guns supplied to merchantmen were modern, suited to the purpose for which they would be required, and manned by a large unit of Naval Reserve gunners under the command of a lieutenant, and including at least two trained signalers. The Richard Hovey was no exception, being armed with two 3-inch dual purpose guns, one mounted forward, the other aft, and eight 20-mm Oerlikons. In the right hands – as it was – this was a formidable armament, giving the Richard Hovey a fire power that would have been coveted by many a British man-of-war.

Twenty-four hours out of Bombay, Radio Officer Mathers, on watch in the Richard Hovey's radio room, picked up an SSS message, relayed through Colombo, from a US merchantman under attack in the Arabian Sea. This was followed some three hours later by a general message broadcast from Bombay warning all Allied ships so equipped, to stream their anti-torpedo nets. Although the horizon was empty as far as the eye could see in any direction, Captain Thorsen knew the enemy was somewhere close at hand.

Thorsen was not wrong. To the north-west of his ship, and moving south-east at all speed, was the Japanese submarine I-26. Commanded by Lieutenant-Commander T. Kusaka, I-26 was one of the Imperial Navy's more successful boats, having gained her first kill within hours of Pearl Harbor, and so earning herself the distinction of being the first Japanese submarine to sink an enemy ship. Thereafter, she operated with continuing success, carrying out an audacious bombardment of Vancouver Island, severely damaging the US carrier Saratoga off the Solomons, and sinking two US light cruisers at Guaducanal. Her score to date was 50,000 tons of Allied shipping, including the 8117-ton Norwegian tanker Grena, sunk off the coast of Oman a few days earlier.

A US Liberty ship in heavy weather

At daylight next morning, 29 March, Chief Officer R.H. Evans turned his deck crew out early to rig the anti-torpedo nets, as advised by Bombay. The A.N.D. (Admiralty Net Defence) equipment, a product of the British Admiralty's "back-room boys," was a recent addition to the defence of Allied merchant ships. It consisted of large steel mesh anti-torpedo nets capable of being lowered into the water on each side of the ship by 50-ft-long booms fitted to her masts. These nets could be streamed while under way, and it was possible to steam at speeds of up to 10 knots with them in place. Providing a ship was not rolling more than 10 degrees, it was claimed the nets gave the vulnerable midships section 50 percent protection against torpedoes. In reality, A.N.D. was, more often than not, a curse which merchant seamen accepted with reluctance. The nets reduced a ship's speed by about 17 percent, hampered her manoeuvrability, and streaming them in anything but the calmest of weather was a herculean and often dangerous task.

Fortunately for Evans and his sailors, the North-East Monsoon still prevailed in the Arabian Sea, and the morning was fine, with the wind blowing light and the sea smooth. Long before sunrise, the Richard Hovey's anti-torpedo nets were in the water and she was steaming along giving a fair imitation of a 7000-ton seine-netter out for a day's fishing.

The Richard Hovey was roughly halfway across the Arabian Sea, and although no ships or aircraft had been seen since leaving Bombay, Thorsen was mindful of the warnings emanating from Colombo and Bombay. His ship was in a state of full alert, with three Armed Guard lookouts stationed in the forward gun tub, three in the after gun tub and two on the bridge. In addition, there was a seaman on lookout in the crow's nest and another on the bridge.

The day passed peacefully, the Richard Hovey maintaining a course of 251 degrees and a speed of 10 knots, despite the drag of her anti-torpedo nets. At 16.00, Chief Officer Evans again took up his watch on the bridge. The weather continued fine and warm, only a light NE'ly breeze ruffling the otherwise placid sea, visibility was good and no alien shape disturbed the horizon. There remained some three hours before darkness fell, meanwhile, Evans made sure the ten lookouts distributed about the ship were fully alert.

Twenty minutes later, the peace of the dying afternoon came to an abrupt end with a cry from the lookout in the starboard wing of the bridge. Speeding towards the ship from a point about 45 degrees on the bow could be seen the tracks of three torpedoes running in parallel. Evans called for hard right rudder, and at the same time, lunged forward to slam the button of the alarm bells with the palm of his hand.

The Richard Hovey began her turn to starboard to comb the path of the approaching torpedoes, but hampered by her heavy nets, she was too slow. One torpedo glided harmlessly past her stern, but the other two caught her amidships, in way of her engine-room and No.4 hold. Her anti-torpedo nets had provided no protection whatsoever.

The two missiles exploded simultaneously, creating carnage in the engine-room and in No.4 cargo hold immediately abaft it. The port boiler blew up, the steering telemotor system was smashed, jamming the rudder hard to port, and all communications throughout the ship were cut. Water poured into the engine-room through the great gash torn in the hull, and oil from the ruptured fuel tanks spilled out to cover the sea with a black, clinging film.

On deck, the havoc created was only marginally less. The combined blast of the torpedoes and the exploding boiler swept up through the engine-room skylight, wrecking the wooden wheelhouse, shearing off ventilators and blowing one of the starboard lifeboats overboard. This was followed by a choking cloud of black smoke and steam which blotted out the sun and added to the chaos. The Richard Hovey took a heavy list to starboard and began to settle by the stern.

Lieutenant Harry Goudy, the Richard Hovey's Armed Guard commander, was in his cabin when the ship reeled under the shock of the triple explosion. Black fumes poured into the cabin, but Goudy escaped suffocation and dashed for his battle station on the bridge. The ship was stopped by the time he reached the bridge, where he found Chief Officer Evans desperately striving to restore order. Captain Thorsen, Goudy discovered, was trapped in his cabin, directly over the port boiler, but was apparently unhurt.

While a squad of seamen, armed with axes, set to work to free Thorsen, Evans ordered the remainder of the crew to clear away the lifeboats and rafts. Meanwhile, Radio Officer Mathers had warmed up his transmitter, which had lain idle for many months, and was doing his utmost to put out an SSS message. His efforts were in vain, for both main and emergency aerials were down.

At 16.40, twenty minutes after the ship had been hit, Captain Thorsen was released from his cabin and arrived on the bridge none the worse for his ordeal. He quickly assessed the damage to the ship as very serious and ordered the boats to be launched. A few minutes later, the Richard Hovey's crew abandoned ship, leaving only Lieut. Goudy and his Armed Guards on board. Thorsen's plan was for the boats to pull clear of the ship to await developments, while Goudy and his men stood to their guns in case the enemy showed himself.

Lieutenant-Commander Kusaka was too experienced to risk his boat by surfacing prematurely, and at 17.00 he put a third torpedo into the Richard Hovey, breaking her back. This forced Goudy to order his gunners to abandon ship, which they did by jumping over the side and swimming to the waiting boats and rafts. When the last man had been picked up, Thorsen took the small flotilla, consisting of three lifeboats and two rafts well clear of the crippled ship.

The engineer and two ratings on watch in the engine-room were missing, presumably killed in the attack. There were also numerous injuries caused by the exploding boiler and flying metal. One of the Armed Guard, Gunner Phillip Fittipaldi, was suffering from serious burns, while the ship's chief engineer, 76-year-old Robert Grey, and one of his oilers, Bjarne Norli, also had burns, but of a less serious nature. The casualty list was high enough, but considering the damage done by the first two torpedoes alone, Thorsen was satisfied it might have been much worse. The question now was how many of them would live to see the land again?

While Thorsen pondered the future and first aid was given to the wounded, a periscope was seen near the ship, which in spite of the terrible beating it had taken, was still afloat. Had they been present, the "Rosie the Riveters" of Portland, Maine would have been proud of their work.

The submarine circled the Richard Hovey for some time before surfacing about 500 yards off her port bow, and under a mile from the lifeboats. She opened fire with her 14-cm deck gun and began to register hits at once. When she ceased fire 12 minutes later, the Liberty was on fire fore and aft. Kusaka then turned his attention to the Richard Hovey's survivors.

The first shell burst close to the boats and all the stories of Japanese atrocities the Americans had heard, but only half-believed, suddenly became very real. The submarine made a wide circle around them, firing all the time, but fortunately not one shell landed near enough to harm the boats or their occupants. When she altered course directly for them and came in with her bow-wave frothing, those survivors who were able needed no urging to take to the water.

When she was some 100 yards off, I-26 opened fire with machine-guns and rifles, spraying the boats and the sea around them. The men in the water scattered and took cover as best they could, some behind the boats and rafts, others striking out, in panic, away from the danger. No.2 boat was rammed and capsized, then the submarine cruised leisurely around, firing indiscriminately at anything that moved. Her casings were crammed with laughing, khaki-clad figures, and above them, in the conning tower, a man with a cine-camera was carefully recording the dreadful scene. At his side stood a tall, dark-skinned individual in a turban. A representative of the self-styled Indian National Army was on hand to witness the humiliation of the white man.

Kusaka again circled wide and brought his 14-cm into use. No.4 lifeboat received a direct hit, but did not sink. Lieutenant Harry Goudy, treading water in the lee of a life raft, quickly cast off the rope attaching his raft to one of the boats when the submarine returned and stopped alongside the boat. Repeated demands for the captain of the ship to show himself went unheeded until threatening gestures were made with rifles and machine-guns. Only then did Thorsen, who was hiding in the bottom of his boat, give himself up. He was taken on board the submarine, along with Second Officer Turner, Able Seaman William Margetko and Fireman Simms, who were also in the boat. The four men disappeared below and I-26 motored off in an easterly direction with the lifeboat in tow.

It was now dusk, and it was essential for the survivors to consolidate their position before darkness fell. There remained only two lifeboats and one raft afloat. Of these, No.2 boat had been rammed and capsized by I-26, and No.4 damaged by a shell, which had, among other things, punctured and emptied the fuel tank, thus rendering the boat's engine useless. Chief Officer Evans took charge of this boat and began picking men out of the water, while Goudy and several others boarded the raft and paddled towards the upturned No.2 boat, rescuing more men as they went. By the time they reached the boat they had sufficient manpower to right it, but it was riddled with bullet holes, fortunately mainly above the waterline, and with many willing hands wielding improvised bailers, it was soon dry. Only then was it discovered that every drinking water tank in the boat had been holed and was near empty. This was a bitter blow.

For the next two hours, with the help of Radio Officer Mathers, Purser James O'Connor and Junior Engineer Arthur Dreschler, Harry Goudy organised a search for more survivors. By 21.00, the last man had been taken from the water and the lifeboat had on board a total of 39, including the badly burned Phillip Fittipaldi. Goudy now held a conference to discuss the options open to them. Owing to the almost total lack of fresh water in the crowded boat, the choice was not wide. It was decided that before any attempt could be made to hoist the sails and make for land, they must return to the Richard Hovey to collect more water. The fires on the ship were visible some miles away, indicating she was still afloat, but as the men were all in an advanced state of exhaustion, it was agreed to wait until daylight before making the attempt.

During the rest of that night, most of them dozed fitfully, while those who could not sleep rowed easily, in order to keep the burning ship in sight. The temperature had dropped rapidly with the going of the sun, and the night was cold and uncomfortable for all. But when dawn finally broke on the 30th, it brought crushing disappointment. At some time during the small hours, the Richard Hovey had succumbed to her grievous wounds and slipped beneath the waves.

An air of complete dejection settled over the boat. The nearest land, the Kathiawar Coast to the north of Bombay, lay 400 miles to the north-east. The wind was too light to even take the creases out of the lifeboat sails, and this was a formidable voyage to attempt under oars alone; without water to drink, it was impossible. As luck would have it, another raft was found with its water tank intact. This would not go far among 39 men, but the find put new heart into them. The two rafts were taken in tow and some of the fitter men transferred to them to ease the overcrowding in the boat. It was decided to steer ENE for Bombay, a distance of nearly 500 miles, and watches were organised for rowing day and night.

Forty-eight hours later, it became clear the boat was making no more than half a knot and the water supply would run out within a few more days, with land still weeks away. Goudy and the other officers put their heads together, and with typical American enterprise, came up with a solution to the crisis. Junior Engineer Arthur Dreschler was given a raft to himself and, possibly drawing on some knowledge handed down to him from the days of prohibition, set about constructing a still from a water tank and various odds and ends from the boat and rafts. Without adequate tools, it was hard and painstaking work, but the still was ready on the 6th. All the woodwork from one raft was then broken up for fuel, and distilling fresh water from salt began. Two days later, when the fuel was used up, 60 gallons of pure water had been produced, sufficient to last for many days to come. The remains of the rafts were then cut adrift, easing the burden of those at the oars. Later, a slight freshening of the wind enabled the sails to be set, and the boat moved eastwards at an encouraging pace.

On the 9th, the condition of Phillip Fittipaldi, whose burns had showed signs of healing, suddenly deteriorated, and he died in the early hours of the 10th. His body was committed to the deep that day in approximately 16 degrees North 67œ degrees East. The passing of Fittipaldi had a profound effect on all those in the boat.

The weather held fine and the boat crept steadily eastwards under sails and oars for the next four days. At about 02.00 on the morning of the 14th, Gunner's Mate, Kuchling, was on watch while the others slept. It was a black night, and for some time Kuchling studied a darker patch on the horizon that could have been a small cloud. He roused Goudy, who examined the horizon through his binoculars and gave an excited shout. It was a ship! Soon the boat was in a ferment. Distress rockets were fired, and Navy Signalmen Smith and Lewis established contact with the ship by means of a torch.

The rescue vessel was, coincidentally, also a Liberty, the British-owned Samuta, commanded by Captain Niblock. In a display of exceptional seamanship, Niblock put his ship alongside the frail lifeboat and all 38 survivors were taken on board. They were landed in Cochin two days later. When discovered by the Samuta, the lifeboat was 280 miles from the Indian coast, having made good 240 miles in an ESE'ly direction in 15 days.

Better luck attended Chief Officer Evans and the 24 men in the Richard Hovey's other lifeboat. They were picked up on 1 April by yet another British Liberty ship, the Samcalia, having made over 200 miles to the east since setting off. They were landed in Karachi on the morning of the 4th.

It is not clear whether Kusaka made a serious attempt to wipe out the survivors of the Richard Hovey, or was merely paying lip service to his Admirals' orders. Certainly, the shelling and machine-gunning of the boats was a deliberate and barbarous act, but it was also singularly ineffective. Not one man was killed or injured in the attack. That no further casualties were suffered was largely due to the dedication of Lieutenant Harry Goudy, gunner turned navigator, and the ingenuity of Junior Engineer Arthur Dreschler, whose improvised distillation plant meant the difference between life and death for 38 men.

I-26 was sunk with all hands to the east of the Phillipines on 17 November 1944 by the escorts USS Lawrence C. Taylor and USS Anzio. Kusaka was not on board at the time.

THIRTEEN

When, on 12 June 1943, 18-year-old Robert Applegate of Michigan enlisted in the United States Naval Reserve, the tide of the Rising Sun had reached its peak in the Pacific and was on the verge of ebbing. Allied forces, recovered from the traumatic shock of the Japanese lightning advances of the previous year, were about to go on the offensive, landings being planned in the Solomons and New Guinea. American submarines, operating from Pearl Harbor and Fremantle, were creating havoc amongst Japanese shipping struggling, to maintain the tenuous supply lines stretching southwards into the furthest reaches of the Pacific. The Imperial Navy had not recovered, nor would it ever, from the death of Admiral Yamamoto and the thorough beating it had taken at Midway. For the Allies the long, hard road to Tokyo had begun.

In early October of that year, after four gruelling months at the Great Lakes Training Station in North Chicago, Robert Applegate emerged as a Seaman First Class and was assigned to the Armed Guard of the US merchantman Jean Nicolet, then in her fitting-out berth at

Portland, Oregon. The Jean Nicolet, a Liberty of 7176 tons, built for the US War Shipping Administration, was under the management of the Oliver J. Olson Steamship Company of San Francisco, and commanded by Captain David Nilsson. She carried a crew of 69, which included 26 Armed Guard gunners and 2 radiomen. In charge of the Guard was Lieutenant Gerald V. Deal, who had at his disposal two 3-inch guns and six 20-mm Oerlikons. The Jean Nicolet was not exactly the fighting ship Robert Applegate had envisaged joining, but she was solid, comfortable, the food was good and the discipline relaxed.

The same could not be said for the Japanese submarine I-8. She was overcrowded, she stank and the food was appalling. But then, when the trees of Northern Oregon shed their leaves at the approach of another winter, I-8 was in the Atlantic, nearing the lonely outpost of St Pauls Rocks and just one degree north of the Equator. Under the command of Captain Shinji Uchino, she was on the return leg of her remarkable voyage to Germany, with every available space in her hull packed with radar equipment, precious metals and spare parts. She also had on board, in addition to her 80-man crew, 12 German radar and hydrophone technicians, whose task, when they reached Japan, would be to remedy some of the serious shortcomings suffered by the boats of the Imperial Navy in the field of detection. I-8 had already been fitted with radar while she was in Germany, but Captain Uchino was not ready to put his trust in this. In order to avoid the attentions of British naval and air patrols, he intended to take his boat 300 miles south of the Cape of Good Hope and into the turmoil of the Roaring Forties, before heading north-east across the Indian Ocean to the Sunda Strait. For I-8 the voyage promised to be long and hazardous. She was not to reach Singapore until early December.

Following her completion at Portland, the Jean Nicolet went south to San Francisco to load her first cargo, destined for Honolulu. Thereafter, she made a second run to Honolulu, and her third voyage took her to New Guinea. By the spring of 1944, she was considered to be a well-tried ship with an experienced crew. In May of that year, she loaded in San Pedro, California, and set out for Calcutta, a port two oceans and half a world away. This was a new departure for her crew, but all the signs were that it would be a trouble-free voyage. In the Pacific, the Allies were on the offensive on all fronts, rolling back the Japanese from island to island, pushing them ever northwards. During the first five months of the year, US submarines had sunk 212 Japanese merchant ships, totalling almost a million tons, and 26 of the enemy's submarines had fallen to a determined Allied campaign. In the Indian Ocean, British flying boats operating from East Africa and Diego Garcia were providing valuable protection for Allied merchant shipping. However, sufficient escort vessels were still not available to convoy ships on the long run from Australia to India, and it was on this route danger lurked underwater in the form of four German and two Japanese submarines. One of the later was the radar-equipped I-8, under the command of Lieutenant-Commander Tatsunosuke Ariizumi, who had so ruthlessly disposed of the Tjisalak and most of her crew in late March.

The Jean Nicolet sailed from San Pedro on 12 May carrying a cargo for the US Army. In her holds were stowed heavy machinery, steel plates and landing craft, while mooring pontoons and unassembled landing barges were lashed down on her open decks. She was to proceed unescorted, first to Fremantle, then to Colombo, and finally to Calcutta, a total voyage of 13,000 miles. Captain David Nilsson was still in command, and with him were Chief Officer Clem Carlin and Chief Engineer James Thurman. Also still in the ship, and about to celebrate his 19th birthday, was Seaman First Class Robert Applegate. On board for the voyage were 30 US Army personnel, swelling the total complement to 100.

Strong adverse winds were experienced on the long run across the Pacific, cutting the Jean Nicolet's average speed back to 9 knots. When Allied troops poured onto the beaches of Normandy on 6 June, she was off New Zealand's north-west point, and it was 20 June, 39 days out of San Pedro, before she finally berthed in Fremantle. The 24 hours spent alongside in the West Australian port, taking bunkers and stores, was a welcome break for the Jean Nicolet's passengers and crew. They were, however, surprised, and not a little disturbed at the apparent total lack of security in the port area. As far as the Australians were concerned the war had now receded to another planet and the port was wide open to visitors. At times, it seemed the whole population of Fremantle had decided to view the ships.

With her fuel tanks and storerooms full, the Jean Nicolet sailed from Fremantle on the 21st and set course for Colombo, 3122 miles to the north-west. The weather was fine and clear, and the Liberty was soon slipping through the long swells at a respectable 10œ knots; a marked change from the frustrations of the Pacific. Some 38 hours out of Fremantle, she picked up the South-East Trades, and with this fair wind behind her, began logging speeds in excess of 11 knots. The hopes for a fast passage were high. The news from the outside world was also encouraging. In the Battle of the Phillipine Sea, the US Pacific Fleet had once again severely thrashed the Imperial Navy, and US Marines had landed in the Marianas. Captain Nilsson had good cause to anticipate a safe arrival at Colombo on or about 8 July.

The first tiny, but ominous cloud appeared on the horizon six days later, when Radioman Cullie Stone, keeping a listening watch in the radio room, picked up a message from Colombo advising a diversion of course to the west. This was prompted by the sinking of the British liner Nellore 500 miles to the north. Tatsunosuke Ariizumi's I-8 was responsible.

On 1 July, the Jean Nicolet passed an empty lifeboat drifting aimlessly. This may, or may not have had some connection with the activities of I-8, but it was certainly a sobering sight. It should also have confirmed for Nilsson that his ship was in an area of great danger. Inexplicably, he postponed the decision to commence zig-zagging for another 48 hours, but he did increase the lookouts and gave orders for the guns' crews to stand-to at dawn and dusk each day.

The morning of the 2nd dawned fine and clear, with only a gentle southerly breeze disturbing the tops of the swells. The Jean Nicolet was 6 degrees south of the Equator, and a long, hot day was in prospect. It was also a day in which Nilsson hoped to sight patrolling flying boats from the British base on Diego Garcia, lying just 150 miles to the west. But when full daylight came, the only object visible on the horizon was the smoke of another vessel, apparently overtaking the Jean Nicolet on her port quarter. Nilsson judged this to be from an American-built "Victory" ship, a larger version of the Liberty notorious for producing billows of black smoke. The word went around that they would soon be sailing in company with another US ship.

Time passed and no ship showed her masts and funnel above the horizon, but throughout the day the low-lying pall of smoke circled the Jean Nicolet, ending up on her starboard bow as the sun went down. Lieutenant Deal took his men to their gun stations as the darkness closed in, relieved by a full, brilliant moon standing high in the sky. The Jean Nicolet's position was 270 miles north-north-east of Diego Garcia; she was steering a course of 357 degrees and making 11.2 knots. At 19.00, with the hour of greatest danger past, Nilsson passed the order for the men to stand down from the guns.

Close to the north-east, trimmed low and hidden in the long swells, I-8 was stealthily manoeuvring into a favourable attack position. In her conning tower, Lieutenant-Commander Ariizumi cursed the persistent clouds of black smoke issuing from the boat's exhausts, threatening to reveal her presence. Being many months away from her base, I-8's hull and engines were sorely in need of attention. The smoke, caused by poor grade diesel taken on at her last re-fuelling at sea, was yet another cross for Ariizumi to bear. Since the sinking of the Tjisalak at the end of March, the pickings had been poor in the Indian Ocean, I-8 having accounted for only the 6589-ton City of Adelaide and an unidentified sailing vessel sunk by gunfire off Adu Atoll. The successful encounter with the Nellore, now known to have been carrying British troops, seemed to indicate a change of fortune, and Ariizumi was anxious to take full advantage of this.

At 19.07, two of Ariizumi's salvo of three torpedoes slammed into the starboard side of the Jean Nicolet one after the other. The first ripped her hull open midway between the bridge and forecastle, while the second burrowed deep into her No.4 hold before exploding. First Assistant Engineer Charles Pyle, on watch in the engine-room, was making an entry in the log book when the first explosion occurred. He was thrown to the plates, but regained his feet quickly and went to the controls to await orders from the bridge. The second explosion, four or five seconds later, again knocked Pyle down, but he was uninjured. No order came from the bridge, and when the ship took a heavy list to starboard, he stopped the engine, shut off the fuel to the boilers, and told the men of his watch to make their way on deck. Then, having satisfied himself all was secure below, he followed them up the ladder.

The wheelhouse was lit up by a flare of yellow light a fraction of a second before the blast swept through it, like a passing express train. Radioman Third Class William Simons, a member of the Armed Guard, on the bridge to deliver a message to Captain Nilsson, was thrown across the wheelhouse, but recovered quickly and rushed aft to the radio room, where he wasted no time in starting up the main transmitter. Seconds later, he was joined by the ship's radio officer Bill

Tilden, who took the key and began sending an SOS. This was immediately answered by Bombay Radio.

Lieutenant-Commander Tatsunoseke Ariizumi,
who sank the Tjisalak and the Jean Nicolet

On being stood down from his gun at 19.00, Robert Applegate went to Lieutenant Deal's office to report. The office was empty, and after waiting a few minutes, Applegate decided to go aft to his quarters. As he passed along the port side of the accommodation, the two heavy explosions occurred. With the alarm bells ringing in his ears and a strong smell of burning in the air, he ran for the nearest gun, an Oerlikon in the port wing of the bridge. As he reached the gun, the ship lurched to starboard and stayed over.

Applegate strapped himself into the Oerlikon and was looking around for a possible target when Lieutenant Deal arrived on the bridge. Deal took over the Oerlikon and ordered Applegate to his normal station at the 3-inch on the forecastle head. The list had by this time increased to 35 degrees and the young gunner had great difficulty in making his way forward along the deck in the darkness. Along the way, he was joined by one of the Jean Nicolet's crew, Ordinary Seaman Floyd Walker. In desperate haste, but awkwardly, owing to the list, the two men loaded the gun then discovered the training mechanism was jammed, probably knocked out of line by the explosions. For some minutes they fought to clear the gun, but to no avail. Realising that, even if the gun could be brought into use, no target was visible, Applegate telephoned the bridge for orders. The reply from the bridge was short and unequivocal; "Abandon ship!"

Captain Nilsson was of the opinion his ship was about to capsize, and when Applegate and Walker reached the boat deck, they found all the lifeboats had left. Nine other men still remained on board, including Captain Nilsson and Lieutenant Deal. While the two senior men made a last round of the ship to look for survivors, Applegate and Walker joined the others in launching a life raft on the port side. When Nilsson and Deal returned, empty-handed, all eleven boarded the raft and pushed off from the ship's side. The sea was then already lapping over the Jean Nicolet's starboard rails.

Despite the suddeness of the attack, the evacuation of the American ship was carried out in an orderly fashion, and within 30 minutes of the order being given. All four lifeboats and two rafts were launched; the rafts on the starboard side were jammed in their chutes and defied release. One of the boats was swamped when it hit the water, but was not damaged and easily bailed out. All 100 men on board left the ship safely, the only casualty being a US Army lieutenant, a passenger in the ship, who fell and broke his arm while boarding his boat.

Soon after leaving the ship, Captain Nilsson transferred to the motor lifeboat and took charge of the situation. No sooner had he done this than gun flashes were seen on the horizon to the north-west and a number of shells slammed into the Jean Nicolet, setting her on fire. Nilsson immediately ordered the boats and rafts to scatter.

Robert Applegate ended up on a raft with Lieutenant Deal and eight others. The raft was heavy and cumbersome, and they could make little progress with the oars. After fifteen minutes of largely fruitless effort, they were forced to give up. As they lay back on their oars, a powerful searchlight stabbed the darkness and the submarine could be seen at about 300 yards. Deal gave the order to go over the side.

Treading water and holding onto the raft's lifelines, Applegate watched the submarine approach the captain's boat. A shrill voice amplified by a megaphone demanded to know the name of their ship. When this had been given, those in the boat were ordered to board the submarine quickly or be shot. Soon after that, Applegate heard a single pistol shot, followed by a burst of machine-gun fire. The warm tropical water around him suddenly took on a deathly chill.

Robert Butler, a 24-year-old seaman first class, was one of the first to board the submarine. He was confronted by a chattering rabble of armed men dressed in khaki uniform with the red flash of the Japanese Imperial Navy on their shoulders. The first act of the Japanese was to summarily execute the young deck boy, William Musser with a single pistol shot to the head. The body of the boy was then kicked overboard like so much garbage, and a machine-gun opened up on the empty lifeboat, riddling it with bullets. A plainer warning that resistance was useless could not have been given.

The stunned American seamen were then relieved of their lifejackets and roughly stripped of watches and rings, before having their hands tied behind their backs. Butler, with a bayonet at his stomach, lost his most treasured possession, a 17-jewelled, yellow gold Bulova wrist watch, before being bundled forward and made to sit crosslegged on the rotting duckboards of the submarine's casing. Already on the casing, sitting three abreast, and facing forward with their hands bound, were twelve or so of the Jean Nicolet's merchant seamen. Most of them had lost their black, Navy-issue leather shoes, to which the Japanese seemed to take a particular fancy. Butler considered himself fortunate to be wearing brown Army GI boots, for which his captors disregarded.

Unaware of the consequence of the shots they had heard, Robert Applegate and his companions remained hidden behind the raft, hoping that they would not be seen. This was not to be. Ariizumi now turned his searchlight on the raft and brought I-8 to within shouting distance. The terrified survivors were told to swim to the submarine or be shot where they were.

Although he had serious misgivings, Applegate had no wish to be a dead hero. He hauled himself aboard the raft and stood up with his hands raised. Four men joined him, but Lieutenant Deal and the remaining four stayed in the water and attempted to drift away out of the light. A machine-gun was turned on them, but none appeared to be hit.

Applegate made the short swim to the submarine and was dragged aboard by two Japanese sailors, both armed with rifles and fixed bayonets. The men used their bayonets to communicate their demands. The gunner was slammed against the conning tower and forced to stand with his hands in the air while his lifejacket was ripped off, followed by his dog tags and watch. He was then spun around and his hands tied securely behind his back, before being marched forward at bayonet point to join those already seated on the casing.

In his immediate vicinity as he was unceremoniously knocked to his knees by a rifle butt, Applegate recognised Captain Nilsson, Chief Officer Carlin, Captain Cussack, US Army, Able Seaman Hess, Able Seaman McDougall, and three members of the Armed Guard, Frank Aten, Robert Nuvill and Raymond Wryozumski. In all, Applegate estimated some thirty survivors were on the foredeck of the submarine. When he ventured to look aft, his curiosity earned him a heavy blow on the back of his neck with an iron bar, but he saw the deck aft was also covered with his erstwhile shipmates, all bound and sitting cross-legged. He was later to learn the Japanese had taken on board 95 of the Jean Nicolet's complement. The only men to escape capture were Lieutenant Deal, Seaman First Class Ora Lamb, Seaman First Class Carl Bevitori, Seaman First Class Raymond Wheeler, and Private Harvey Matthias of the US Army. All had swum away from the raft when Applegate had surrendered.

When all other survivors were on board and made secure, I-8's diesels were started up and she circled around, firing on the abandoned boats and rafts with her machine-guns. The deck was cleared away in the region of the twin 14-cm guns and several rounds were fired at the Jean Nicolet. This gave the Japanese guards pleasure in forcing the American prisoners to watch their ship being pounded. While this was going on, Carl Rosenbaum, an engine-room rating, and the injured Army lieutenant were washed overboard by the submarine's bow wave. Both men were bound, but no effort was made to save them.

It was around midnight when a Japanese officer, complete with Samauri sword, moved among the prisoners demanding the captain and officers declare themselves. There was silence, followed by the usual death threats, then Captain Nilsson and Chief Officer Carlin stood up. Applegate watched them being taken aft to the conning tower, along with Radio Officer Bill Tilden, who had been foolish enough to put on his best uniform before abandoning ship. The three men were not seen again.

The subsequent treatment of the survivors of the Jean Nicolet then followed the same pattern of mindless brutality which has become all too familiar. One by one, the Americans, mentally and physically drained by their long ordeal, were led abaft the conning tower and forced to run the gauntlet of a double line of grinning Japanese armed with clubs, bayonets and swords. First Assistant Engineer Charles Pyle later described his own experience.

"Somewhere around midnight, I was picked up and led aft, at which time I noticed the deck guns being secured and that 30 or 35 survivors of our vessel were still sitting on the submarine deck. I learned then that the Japanese were employing a tactic similar to the old Indian practice of running the gauntlet, wherein they force survivors to pass between two lines of men armed with clubs, bars and other blunt instruments, and, when reaching the end, being either shoved or knocked into the sea to drown. Apparently this process had been going on for some time before I was called to take my turn and I estimate that approximately sixty people had been handled in this fashion prior to my adventure. Then I was led to the front of two lines, composed of Japanese crew members, facing one another and forming the gauntlet line, with approximately eight men on the inboard line and four or five on the outboard. When I momentarily stopped to survey the situation, I was struck a terrific blow at the base of my head which caused me to feel a sensation similar to a bouncing ball. From there on I was shoved down through the two lines of Japanese who rained blows upon my body and head with various objects which I was too stunned and dazed to identify, although I was later advised by my doctor that I had been cut with a bayonet or sword in the process. When I reached the end of the gauntlet, I fell into what appeared to be a white foamy sea."

Seaman First Class Robert Butler added to this.

"Soon they came and got me and took me back aft where eight or ten Japs were lined up against the conning tower holding sabres, clubs and lengths of lead pipe. One Jap stopped me and tried to kick me in the stomach. Another hit me over the head with an iron pipe. Another cut me over the eye with a sabre. I managed to break away after I had gotten past the second one and jumped overboard, and although I did not lose consciousness the sub had gone when I came up, but was still in sight."

Robert Applegate had been sitting cross-legged on the hard duck boards for almost three hours, the ropes that bound him were cutting into his wrists, and his head ached from the blows he had received. He was not clear about the fate of the men being taken aft, but was aware none of them had returned. He had resigned himself to await his turn when the sound of alarms bells came from inside the submarine and events took a dramatic turn. Within seconds, all the Japanese guards disappeared below, there was a loud rush of air, and the bow tilted downwards. The submarine was crash diving.

Those left on the casings, thirty men or more, struggled to their feet in blind panic. With their hands securely bound, it was certain they would drown. But every crisis has its "man of the hour," and this time it was Able Seaman George Hess, who had been secretly working on his bonds for some time, and had broken free at the crucial moment. Fortunately, Gunner's Mate Stanley Wryozumski, who despite being searched by the Japanese, had held onto his pocket knife. Using this knife and working with desperate haste, for the deck was rapidly sinking beneath his feet, Hess moved quickly from man to man slashing at their bonds. He had freed half a dozen by the time the suction of the diving submarine dragged them all down.

Applegate's bonds were only partly cut, but he was able to break free as he went under. Kicking clear of the submarine, he came to the surface to find a sea of heads bobbing around him. He tried to loosen the ropes binding the nearest man, Deck Engineer Paul Mitchem, but his fingers were numb and clumsy. After a brief struggle he gave up and swam off to get help.

As he swam around, Applegate called to the others, but most had their own problems to grapple with, the few who were free striving to help their less fortunate shipmates. The situation seemed completely without hope. Then Applegate saw a sight which caused him to rub his eyes in disbelief. Skimming low over the water in the direction of the Jean Nicolet were the red and green navigation lights of an aircraft. It was this plane, a Catalina of the Royal Canadian Air Force, appearing in answer to Radio Officer Tilden's SOS, that must have caused Ariizumi to crash dive before his bloody night's work was done. Ironically, the German radar fitted to I-8 at the time Robert Applegate joined the Jean Nicolet, had been instrumental in saving the young seaman from a horrible death.

Soon after the aircraft flew away again, Applegate met up with Seaman First Class Robert Butler and Utilityman Harold Lee. Butler's hands were still bound, and the ropes so swollen by the water the others could not release him. With Butler supported between them, Applegate and Lee set off to swim to the Jean Nicolet, some two miles away. If they did not reach the ship, or find some wreckage to keep them afloat, they would perish.

Dawn came, and to the three exhausted men the ship appeared as far away as ever, but they kept going. Two and a half hours later, they were still swimming when the Jean Nicolet slipped under the waves stern first. If they had been capable of tears, they would have shed them. Having been in the water for eight hours, to see their only hope of salvation suddenly disappear was a crushing blow. Applegate broke away from the others and swam around aimlessly, his emotions numbed. He came across Chief Engineer James Thurman, who with the aid of two wooden paddles, was swimming towards the ship that was no more. When Applegate called to him, Thurman took no notice and continued swimming on, into oblivion.

Thereafter, Applegate met a number of other survivors, all swimming hopefully towards a ship that no longer existed. A change in his luck came when he found two small wooden crates. These did not have sufficient buoyancy to keep him afloat, but they were something tangible to hold on to; a tenuous link with the real world he felt was slipping away. Then Radioman William Simons drifted by. He was in such poor shape Applegate swam across to him and offered to share his precious crates. The two men decided to stay together to await what ever fate had in store for them.

Sometime during that day – such was the state of their minds it could have been morning or afternoon – Applegate and Simons saw a number of low-flying aircraft searching the area, but none came near them. When the sun went down, it grew bitterly cold and both men, near to delirium, floated in a fantasy world. Around midnight, they saw a searchlight sweeping the sea and the terror of the Japanese submarine came back to haunt them. Mercifully, Applegate lost consciousness. When, soon after sunrise on the 4th, he was roused by the sting of a jellyfish, Simons had gone.

The Fourth of July 1944 proved to be an Independence Day Robert Applegate would never forget. At about noon, he looked up from his hopeless reverie to find a Catalina circling low overhead. A dark object dropped from the underside of the plane, a parachute opened, and a small inflatable raft landed in the water alongside him. He boarded the raft with difficulty, but with his heart soaring. A few minutes later, a ship appeared, and within half an hour he was in the sick bay of His Majesty's Indian Ship Hoxa. When he was rescued, Robert Applegate had been in the water for 34 hours without a life-jacket.

By 15.00 that day, HMIS Hoxa had picked up 23 survivors, all that remained of the 100 who sailed out of San Pedro in the Jean Nicolet. The others, including Captain David Nilsson, Chief Officer Clem Carlin, Chief Engineer James Thurman and Radio Officer Bill Tilden, were either shot or bayoneted aboard I-8, drowned with their hands tied, or taken by sharks.

On 31 March 1945, I-8 was sunk off Okinawa by the US destroyers Morrison and Stockton. Only one man survived. But Ariizumi had already moved on. He was at that time commanding a squadron of new 3500-ton boats working up in the Inland Sea for an attack on the Panama Canal. The war ended before the attack could be made. Tatsunoseke Ariizumi, moved either by shame or defiance, shot himself while taking the squadron back to Yokosuka to surrender to the Allies at the end of August that year.

FOURTEEN

The early evening fog was rolling in through the Golden Gate when, on 24 October 1944, the John A. Johnson sailed from San Francisco. Loaded to her maximum draught of 28 feet, the 7176-ton Liberty carried in her holds 6,900 tons of provisions and 150 tons of ammunition, the latter distributed equally between her No.1 and 5 holds, both sited well away from her accommodation. On deck, every available square foot of space was covered by Army trucks, crated and uncrated. The John A. Johnson, operated by the American Mail Line, and under charter to the US Navy, was going to war. In command was 41-year-old Captain Arnold Beeken, and her total complement was 70, including the usual 28-strong contingent of the Armed Guard and an Army Cargo Security Officer.

Once through the narrows of San Francisco Bay, Captain Beeken saw his pilot over the side and rang for full speed. His orders were to take the heavily-laden ship with all dispatch to Honolulu, where her final destination would be revealed; this being a not unusual proce-dure in wartime. Beeken felt safe in assuming the voyage would end many thousands of miles to the west of the Hawaiian Islands, for the war in the Pacific was moving that way with a fierce momentum.

For the Japanese, the bitter taste of defeat began with the fall of Saipan, in the Marianas, on 9 July. This precipitated the suicide of Admiral Nagumo, the resignation of General Tojo's entire cabinet, and air attacks on Tokyo and other main cities by B 29's of the US Air Force. The bombs were a tremendous psychological blow to Japan's civilian population, which had hitherto believed its island home to be impregnable. For them a bloody war of attrition was now in progress; a war that could have only one end.

By the middle of August, with the exception of a few isolated pockets of resistance, the Marianas were entirely in American hands, and there, momentarily, the onward march stopped. A secure base was now needed from which to mount the final assault on the Japanese mainland. One powerful school of thought favoured Formosa, but General Douglas MacArthur, anxious to avenge his humiliating retreat from these islands in January 1942, pressed for a return to the Phillipines. MacArthur won the argument, and US troops stormed ashore at Leyte on 20 October. In their wake the supply ships began anchoring off the beaches, and it seemed most likely the John A. Johnson was destined to join them.

Three days out of San Francisco, on the afternoon of the 27th, the weather deteriorated rapidly, the wind rising from the west, accompanied by a long northerly swell. The barometer was falling quickly and Captain Beeken knew from past experience one of the Pacific's periodical hurricanes must be passing, some 200 miles or so to the north of his ship. Fortunately, at this distance the awesome power of the storm would be much reduced. The wind was unlikely to rise above force 6, but the swell moving outwards from the eye of the storm like ripples from a stone tossed into a pond, could be a problem for the John A. Johnson. With this swell on the beam, and a westerly wind whipping up a head sea, the passage to Honolulu promised to be an uncomfortable one.

By the time darkness came, the John A. Johnson was plunging her rounded bows into a heavy sea and shipping water over her forecastle head. For an ocean-going ship of her size, this was hardly threatening, but the swell was another matter. The Liberty ship, with her heavy cargo of trucks on deck, was in nautical terms "tender," meaning that, with insufficient bottom weight to balance the deck cargo, she had a tendency to roll excessively. Coming in long and high from the north, and catching the ship square on her starboard beam, the swell gave her a pendulum-like motion that was both stomach-churning and dangerous. There were times when, caught in a cycle of ever increasing rolls, the John A. Johnson rolled her main deck rails under. Those on watch struggled to keep their feet, while the marginally luckier ones, below, wedged themselves into their bunks in a futile effort to sleep. Life on board became a wearisome round, and it was to stay that way until the hurricane spiralled its way across the ocean and out of range.

At sometime during that night, a heavy swell climbed aboard and carried away a life raft stowed in a quick-release cradle between No.4 and 5 hatches. The loss was discovered in the early hours of the 28th, and Beeken at once ordered Radio Officer Gorden Brown to transmit a message reporting the loss to the nearest shore station. In peacetime this is standard practice, designed to pre-empt an unnecessary rescue operation being mounted, should an empty raft be sighted. During the Second World War, when the oceans were at times littered with drifting rafts and lifeboats, occupied and unoccupied, this action was not considered necessary. In retrospect, it is difficult to understand why Captain Beeken took the risk of breaking radio silence. As it was, Brown had difficulty in contacting the shore and continued to transmit on 468 kilocycles for a full 12 minutes before the message was passed.

It was unfortunate for the John A. Johnson that, at the time her radio officer was transmitting, the Japanese submarine I-12 happened to be within range, and on the surface, recharging her batteries. I-12, commanded by Lieutenant-Commander Kaneo Kudo, was a new 2200-ton, long-range patrol boat, armed with one 14-cm gun, several light machine-guns, 18 torpedoes and a spotter aircraft. Additionally, she was equipped with a German-built radar and a high performance radio direction finder. However, despite having scoured the Pacific assiduously for more than three months, I-12 had yet to claim her first kill. Undoubtedly, it was of considerable satisfaction to Kudo when, early on the 28th, his operator picked up and zeroed in on the John A. Johnson's transmision.

During the hours of daylight on the 28th, the weather showed a steady improvement, until by nightfall the wind had dropped to force 3-4, and the clouds rolled back to reveal a bright moon three-quarters full. But there was no let-up in the heavy beam swell, and the John H. Johnson continued to roll her rails under. She was steering a course of 239 degrees and making 8.9 knots. Honolulu lay a thousand miles over the western horizon.

A few minutes before 21.00, Captain Beeken appeared on the bridge and went through his customary nightly routine, of checking all was well with the navigation. Third Officer Van Barber had the watch, and with him were a helmsman, a lookout man, and four Armed Guard gunners standing by at the Oerlikons, in each wing of the bridge. Two of the gunners would normally have been in the forward gun tub, but owing to the amount of green water being shipped over the bow, the bridge was deemed a far safer place for them to keep their watch.

Having compared the standard and steering compasses and briefly studied the ship's position on the chart, Beeken moved out into the port wing to join Third Officer Barber. The two men, their legs spread wide against the never-ending roll of the ship, stood talking for a while, discussing the voyage ahead. As they talked, their eyes instinctively searched the horizon from ahead to the beam, but it was from their blind side that the sudden and vicious attack came. At approximately 21.05, the ship took a heavy roll to port and I-12's torpedo slammed into her exposed starboard underwater plating, immediately forward of the bridge.

The violent explosion tore a huge hole in the John A. Johnson's hull, but its upward thrust was smothered by the tightly packed cases of canned provisions in her No.3 hold. Only minor damage was done to the bridge house. Beeken recovered from the shock quickly and dived into the wheelhouse, where he swung the engine-room telegraph to "Stop." As an afterthought, in case anyone might not be aware of the emergency visited upon them, he sounded the General Alarm on the ship's bells. His next move was to telephone the radio room.

In the radio room, a dazed Gorden Brown picked himself up from the deck, where he had been thrown by the explosion. He was bleeding from a cut above his right eye, but was able to acknowledge Beeken's order to send an SSS, together with the ship's position. Unfortunately, as Brown reached out to start up the main transmitter, the lights dimmed and then died altogether. Below decks, the steam lines to the generators had been severed, wiping out all electrical power.

At first, unsure of the extent of the damage, Beeken considered the possibility of saving his ship. But the angle of the deck increased and the ominous grinding of steel on steel, coming from forward of the bridge, indicated the torpedo had broken the John A. Johnson's back. With the heavy swell wracking her, it could only be a matter of time before she broke up. Reluctantly, Beeken reached for the whistle lanyard and sounded the Abandon Ship signal.

Meanwhile, Gorden Brown, having made a quick dash to his cabin for his lifejacket and a torch, returned to the radio room, where he met one of the Armed Guard radiomen. Working with as much haste as they could, the two operators set up the battery-powered emergency transmitter and switched on. The motor functioned perfectly, but when the key was pressed, no power registered on the aerial meter. It was almost certain the aerials were down, but in case the meter itself was damaged and not registering, Brown perservered, sending the standard SSS message and the ship's position of 29° 55'N 141° 25'W, as passed to him by the bridge. He completed the first transmission just as the urgent blaring of the ship's whistle told she was about to be abandoned. The question of whether or not his transmissions were going out over the air had become academic. Brown closed the station down and called to the Navy radioman to accompany him to the bridge. Their top priority now was to make sure the portable radio transmitter, kept on the bridge, went into a lifeboat.

Third Officer Barber was also preparing to leave the ship for the last time. Keeping a tight grip on his nerves, he called first at the chartroom to pick up a sextant and chronometer, then collected his lifejacket from his cabin two decks below. The return journey, through darkened alleyways strewn with obstacles, seemed to be endless. When he finally gained the boat deck, Barber found most of the crew already assembled in orderly groups. The forward starboard boat was badly damaged and could not be lowered, but the three others appeared intact. Barber directed his attention to the lowering of No.2 boat, of which he would be in charge. The exaggerated rolling of the ship made the launch extremely difficult, but this was accomplished, and the third officer and his crew boarded and pulled away.

Radio Officer Brown, assigned to No.3 boat, did not have such an easy time. The boat was lowered to the water successfully, but when Brown boarded with the portable radio transmitter, it became clear that this boat had been holed during the torpedoing. As the men piled in, it began to sink, and there was a hurried exodus over the gunwales. Brown was most reluctant to leave his radio, which could be the means of saving all their lives. He stayed with the boat until it was completely waterlogged, and only then did he join the others in the water.

Being satisfied that, to the best of his knowledge, all his men had left the ship, Captain Beeken went below to collect confidential papers and code books from the safe in his cabin. His journey was in vain, for the fore part of the John A. Johnson's accommodation block was wide open to the sea, a dark, empty space filled with the eerie sound of the broken ends of the ship clashing together. Beeken turned back, but before he left, searched the accommodation for anyone who might be left behind. He drew a blank amidships, and then went aft to check the Armed Guards' quarters. To his amazement, he found four gunners still manning the after gun, all oblivious to the fact that the ship had been abandoned. As Beeken spoke to the men, the John A. Johnson broke in two, the section forward of the bridge drifting away, while the after part, on which they stood, tipped heavily by the stern. Fearful that capsize would soon follow, Beeken and the gunners ran to the rails and dived overboard.

It was by a stroke of the purest luck that the five swimmers found the abandoned No.3 lifeboat, which was awash and floating on its buoyancy tanks. Grateful for small mercies on a night so full of horror, they scrambled aboard. Ten minutes later, they picked up three others. Seated, waist-deep in water and surrounded by darkness, there was then little the eight men could do but wait for daylight.

Gorden Brown and the others, who had evacuated the waterlogged boat, were taken on board by Third Officer Barber, making the complement of his boat up to 28. Soon after they boarded, the boat drifted close to the starboard side of the stern section of the John A.

Johnson, and narrowly escaped being crushed by the bow section, which bore down on them out of the night. With seconds to spare, they shipped the oars and pulled clear, to join up with the two other boats and a life raft.

It was now clearly established that all 70 men had abandoned the John A. Johnson without injury, a remarkable feat considering the circumstances prevailing. Half an hour later their luck ran out. Kaneo Kudo brought I-12 to the surface, and after scanning the sea and sky for possible danger, motored towards the boats at full speed.

Barber was first to see the approaching submarine and urged his crew to jump over the side. Most followed his advice at once, and those who were not quick enough were thrown into the water when I-12 deliberately rammed the boat. Providentially, the blow was only a glancing one, but Kudo opened fire with a machine-gun. Gorden Brown, hidden behind the boat, watched the huge, black-painted submarine glide past, her tracers sweeping the surrounding sea. A figure in white uniform, whom he assumed to be the commander, was visible in the conning tower, at his side, two men in khakis, wielding pistols. On the casings were 10 or 15 others, whose screams of "Banzai!" accompanied each fusillade of machine-gun fire. The brutish enjoyment of the Japanese at the killing was incomprehensible.

The slaughter went on for 45 terrible minutes, Kudo adopting the usual procedure of weaving through and around the boats, ramming where possible, and using machine-guns and the submarine's screws to blot out all traces of the John A. Johnson's crew. The life raft, with 17 survivors on board, was found and given similar treatment. The screams of the dying mingled on the night air with the obscene cries of their executioners.

At last, Kudo grew tired of the killing and returned to finish off the John A. Johnson, the two broken sections of which were lying about a quarter of a mile apart. He narrowed the range to 2000 yards and opened up with his 14-cm. Four hits were scored, setting both hulks on fire. I-12 then made one final run between the lifeboats, causing those who had reboarded to take to the water again. There was no firing this time, but for the next two hours the survivors watched in trepidation as the submarine cruised, menacingly, in the vicinity. They feared she was waiting for daylight to finish them off.

For the passengers on board the Pan American Airways flying boat, four hours out from San Francisco and bound for Honolulu, time was dragging. The flight was bumpy and sleep impossible. Endless cups of coffee and chain-smoked cigarettes dulled the nerves, but produced only a sense of suspended animation that just made the journey bearable. Then, suddenly, just after 01.00 on the 30th, the interior of the plane came alive. Far below, on that great expanse of moonlit emptiness they knew to be the sea, could be seen first one, then two winking fires. The pilot dropped lower, and soon the two burning halves of a ship were clearly visible. Near by was a tiny cluster of lifeboats, and beyond that the unmistakeable shape of a submarine crouched on the surface like a predator waiting for the right moment to kill. This was a never-to-be-forgotten sight, made all the more memorable when the forward half of the John A. Johnson, containing 70 tons of ammunition, blew apart, sending flames 700 feet into the air.

The captain of the flying boat circled low and made contact with one of the lifeboats by signal lamp. The news of the fate of the John A. Johnson was passed to San Francisco without delay, and before long a rescue operation had been initiated. The aircraft carrier USS Argus, cruising 90 miles away from the scene, had heard the explosion and was already on the alert. As soon as she received a position from San Francisco, the carrier headed towards the spot at full speed.

At 08.00, aircraft from the Argus finally located the survivors and parachuted down a portable radio transmitter. When this was retrieved and rigged, it took only minutes to contact the carrier. USS

Argus arrived at 14.00 and took on board 60 survivors from the John A. Johnson, many of whom had bullet wounds or injuries sustained when the boats were rammed. They were landed at San Francisco on 3 November.

I-12 had, of course, long since disappeared from the scene of her crime when the US planes arrived. Behind her she left the bodies of 10 American seamen floating face down in the sea. They had survived the sinking of their ship, but not the malice of Kaneo Kudo's bullets.

The ultimate fate of I-12 is not clear. One report says she disappeared with all hands in Pacific waters in January 1945, another that she was sunk off Okinawa by US carrier-borne aircraft in May of that year. The John A. Johnson was her only recorded victim.

EPILOGUE

Early on the morning of 6 August 1945, a US Army Air Force B-29 Superfortress circled 5 miles high over the Japanese port city of Hiroshima and released the first atomic bomb ever to be used in war. In the space of a few minutes an awesome destructive power, equivalent to 20,000 tons of TNT, wiped out 150,000 men, women and children. Three days later, a second bomb fell on Nagasaki and a further 40,000 died. In the years that followed, thousands more were to succumb to the lasting effects of these bombs. Many, if not most, of those who suffered were innocent of any active participation in the Second World War, and their suffering must be regretted. But, as a deterrent the atom bomb had no equal. Eight days after Hiroshima, on 14 August 1945, Japan surrendered unconditionally to the Allies. The war in the Far East, one of the most bitter in history, was over at last.

There are those who say the atom bomb should never have been used; that the Japanese did not deserve the dreadful retribution of Hiroshima and Nagasaki. They will argue that Japan was already beaten, her main cities in ruins, her great navy crushed, and her only allies, Italy and Germany, long finished. It should then have been a relatively simple matter for Allied forces to mount a complete blockade of the islands and starve them into surrender. Some go even further and say the Americans used the bombs to exact a fearful revenge for the humiliating defeats the Japanese inflicted on them in the early stages of the war in the Pacific. There may be some justification in both these claims, but in avoiding the necessity for a long blockade or a direct assault on Japan, the bombs probably saved a million lives, Allied and Japanese. One thing is certain – although there are still many who will not agree – the demonstration of the immense power of the nuclear bomb at Hiroshima and Nagasaki in 1945 served to condemn global war to the history books for ever.

It was long after the end of the war that I first came to know the Japanese – a quarter of a century later, when their country was in the throes of a white-hot industrial and technological revolution, which led to the almost unchallenged commercial supremacy they enjoy today. I found the Japanese to be, in the main, a likeable, conscientious and hard-working people. The exaggerated politeness they display towards each other, and to outsiders, which I had always assumed to be false, I discovered to be often quite genuine. In their society there is a great respect for law and order, a marked lack of gratuitous violence, scrupulous attention to cleanliness, and due regard to the wisdom that age brings. Their tight organisation and attention to detail commands my admiration, as does their ability to play as hard as they work. Over the years, I made many friends in Japan, and find it hard to come to terms with the fact that among them may have been some who were associated with, or even responsible for some of the dreadful atrocities committed against Allied merchant seamen in the years 1941 to 1945.

The bestial treatment meted out to Allied prisoners of war on the Burma Road, in Changi Jail, and in the jungle camps of Java and Sumatra is well documented and unlikely to ever be forgotten. Likewise, the torture and mass slaughter of the indigenous population of many of the lands the Japanese occupied. But who remembers the men of the Daisy Moller, the Behar, the Tjisalak and the Jean Nicolet? What retribution was exacted for their anguish and subsequent murder?

In Tokyo in May 1946, the United Nations opened a great show trial of the Japanese accused of war crimes. It lasted until November 1948 and provided lucrative employment for many thousands of lawyers, officials and hangers-on. During the two and a half years whilst the court sat, 5,500 were accused of killing, torturing, or otherwise ill-treating Allied servicemen and civilians. Of those on trial, 4,450 were found guilty and 1000 suffered death by hanging. For many, justice had been seen to be done. As for those whose stories fill these pages, their deaths went almost unnoticed and unavenged.

Lieutenant Y. Kayahara, who set the stage by the ruthless killing by machine-gunning of 27 of the Donerail's crew in December 1941, was never brought to trial. Lieutenant-Commander S. Kitamura, who so diligently murdered 79 of the crew of the Langkoeas on that evil night in the Java Sea in January 1942, and may have, in like manner disposed of the entire crew of the Boero, did not answer for his crimes. Lieutenant-Commander H. Nakagawa, that stranger to compassion responsible for the deaths of 296 men and women whose only warlike act was to sail in the hospital ship Centaur, who machine-gunned survivors of the British Chivalry, the Sutlej and the Ascot, killing a further 103, also disappeared from view when the war ended. There was no accurate count of the number of the Nancy Moller's men Lieutenant T. Shimizu murdered, on a tranquil March morning, to the south of Ceylon, but it was certainly in excess of 20. However, when the day of reckoning came after the war, Shimizu could not be found to answer his accusers. Did anyone bother to look for him? The same applies to Lieutenant-Commander Kaneo Kudo, who ruthlessly disposed of 10 of those who survived the sinking of the John A. Johnson. Commander Tamatso Oishi of the Aikoku Maru murdered only three of the Ondina's survivors, while Lieutenant-Commander T. Kusaka who sank the Richard Hovey, used his machine-guns on men in the water, but killed none. Both might conceivably have been found guilty of acting in the heat of the moment and without real intent, had they been brought to trial – which, of course, they were not.

It was not necessary to bring before the courts Lieutenant Kazuro Ebato, perpetrator of the Daisy Moller massacre, in which 55 died by his machine-guns. He received swift justice at the hands of the Royal Navy when RO-110 was sunk with all hands two months later. Lieutenant-Commander Tatsunoseke Ariizumi, who ruthlessly slaughtered 97 men and one woman of the Dutch ship Tjisalak, and later similarly disposed of 77 survivors of the American Liberty Jean Nicolet, died by his own hand. He thus escaped justice and, by his own perverted standards, gained immortality.

In the end, only four men appeared before the court in Tokyo charged with crimes against Allied merchant seamen. Vice-Admiral Naomasa Sakonju and Captain Haruo Mayazumi were charged with, and found guilty of, murder by beheading of 72 of the Behar's crew and passengers. Sakonju was sentenced to death and hanged. Mayazumi, whose Christian upbringing prompted him to protest against the mass execution, received only seven years in jail. Two officers who were in I-8 at the time of the Tjisalak massacre, Lieutenant Sadao Monontaka and Lieutenant Masanori Hattori, also stood trial in Tokyo and were given seven and five years imprisonment respectively.

Such was the miserly payment exacted for the wilful murder of more than 800 defenceless souls. One wonders what Horatio Nelson would have thought of the whole dirty business.

I cannot end this book without remarking on the number of occasions on which the merchant ships concerned were encouraged to break radio silence, by those who should have known better. There is no direct evidence that the Japanese submarines used these transmissions, some of them ridculously prolonged, to home in on their victims, but I am convinced this must have happened in some cases.

BIBLIOGRAPHY

BEZEMER, K.W.L., De Geschiedenis van de Nederlandse Koopvaarij in de Tweede Wereldoorlog.

BLAIR, CLAY, Silent Victory (Bantam Books 1975)

BRYANT, ARTHUR, The Turn of the Tide (Collins 1957)

CHURCHILL, W.S., The Second World War (Cassell 1948-52)

COSTELLO, JOHN, The Pacific War (Collins 1981)

DEVA, JAYA, Japan's Kampf (Gollanz 1942)

FISCHER, LOUIS, The Story of Indonesia (Harperf 1959)

FALLS, CYRIL, The Second World War (Methuen 1948)

HASHIMOTO, MOCHITSURA, Sunk (Cassell 1954)

HOWARTH, STEPHEN, Morning Glory (Hamilton 1983)

ISHIMARU, TOTA, Japan Must Fight Britain (Hurst & Blackett 1936)

ROHWER, JURGEN, Axis Submarine Successes 1939-1945 (Patrick Stephens 1983)

ROSKILL, CAPT. S.W., The War at Sea (HMSO 1954-61)

RUSSELL OF LIVERPOOL, LORD, The Knights of Bushido (Cassell 1958)

STORRY, RICHARD, A History of Modern Japan (Cassell 1960)

THOMAS, DAVID, Battle of the Java Sea (Deutsch 1968)

VON MUNCHING, L.L., De Nederlandse Koopvaarrdijvloot in de Tweede Wereldoorlog.

WHITEHOUSE, ARCH, Subs and Submariners (Doubleday 1961)

ZAINUDDIN, AILSA, A Short History of Indonesia (Cassell 1968)

ACKNOWLEDGEMENTS

The author gratefully acknowledges the valuable assistance given to him in the research for this book by the following sources and people:

Public Record Office, Kew; General Register and Record Office of Shipping and Seamen, Cardiff; National Archives, Washington D.C.; Welsh Industrial and Maritime Museum, Cardiff; Ministry of Defence, Naval Staff Duties, London; The St Ives Museum; Mrs D. Barker, K.W.L. Bezemer, Lord James Blears, Gus Britton, Sheila Bywater, Bernard E. Cavalcante, Mrs E. Cawkwell, William Coxe, W.L. Griffiths, Captain Samuel Crowther, James Cuthbert, Frank Darley, Mrs H. Duff, Mrs Jean Eaton, W.T. Evans, Michael Kaufmann, S. Lawford, Jack Matthews, Lewis Maxwell-Clarkson, David J. Morris, Captain Pierre Payne, Mrs Betty Phillips, Mrs M.M. Rees, Mrs D. Rowlandson, Richard A. von Doenhoff, and in particular, Frits Noorbergen of Amstelveen, without whose help I would have had great difficulty in reconstructing the incidents concerning the Dutch ships.

INDEX

INDEX

INDEX

INDEX

INDEX

INDEX

INDEX

INDEX

INDEX

INDEX

SHIPS

SHIPS continued,

Brick Tower Press
1230 Park Avenue
New York, NY 10128, US
1-800-68-BRICK
bricktower@aol.com

For sales, editorial information,
subsidiary rights information or a catalog,
please write or phone or e-mail.

In the United Kingdom contact
New Guild
73 Wollaton Road
Ferndown, Dorset BH22 8QS
Tel/Fax: (01202) 897614